The Life of A Real Woman, Real But Healed

By: Author Carol Godfrey

Bailey Girls Publishing LLC
www.baileygirls.com

The Life of A Real Woman, Real But Healed
Copyright © 2020 Carol Godfrey

All rights reserved. No portion of this book may be reproduced, stored in a retrieval system, or transmitted in any form or by any means—electronically, mechanically, photocopy, recording, scanning, or otherwise—except for brief quotations in critical reviews or articles, without the prior written permission of the author.

Printed in the United States of America

ISBN 978-194203708-8

For book orders, author appearances, inquiries, speaking engagements and/or interviews, please contact the author by email at:

carolgodfrey1206@gmail.com

Printed in United States of America

Published by Bailey Girls Publishing LLC

BaileyGirls.com

Dedication

To my awesome husband and wonderful friend. To the One who believed in me when I wasn't sure of myself. To the One who "inspired me;" to the One who made it possible, my Comforter, best friend, Jesus. I'll love you until death do I part from Earth to Glory.

Acknowledgements

To Apostle Moore and Elder Dorothy. When all other leaders couldn't see what you saw and heard, who wanted this "sheep to prosper," multiply, and replenish women like me, thank you, thank you, thank you.

To the Doors of Faith Partners, God did it for me through you. Thank you for the spiritual and financial support. Reach for your dreams and vision.

To my mother who gave her life, her home, her vehicles, her finances while I was on this spiritual faith ride. I owe you for the rest of my life. I love you dearly.

To my daughter, Sierra, Grandkids, Ayden, Samiyah, and Baby Jordan, I love you to life. You all are my life, after Jesus.

My sister, Phyllis, my brothers, Clarence and Charles, God did it. Love you all to life.

To my bone-in, sisters and brothers in Christ, Sally, Rhonda, Tyrone, Prophet Perkins, Sis Melinda, Donna, Phyllis White, Sharonda, Karen, Shirley Freshwater, Teresa Ross, and DaVia Purnell.

A special thank you to my niece, SeLisa Godfrey, who took time to type for me; you know I didn't know how to put this project together. I am so grateful and thankful to you.

To Mrs. Barbara Judd who gave her knowledge and wisdom to me, and took the time to work hard typing my manuscript for me, while dealing with her own struggles and battles, with sickness and death in her family. Thank you, thank you from the bottom of my heart.

To Pastor Antonio Williams, thank you for allowing God to use you, to help me. Thank you, thank you!

To "Cuz" Clyndell Godfrey, thank you for being there for me when I needed you the most. Thank you, thank you!

To Dad and Mom Butts, thank you for standing by me through thick and thin. I love ya'll to life.

To Paige Old Photography, thank you for the professional photo that you took of me; you captured the moment. Sis, thank you, thank you!

To Tabitha Harris, when it seemed as though nothing was going right with **the cover,** God gave me you. Thank you so much.

This is my life - The Life of A Real Woman, Real But Healed.

Table of Contents

A Quick Look 1
Just When You Think 3
The Reason 4
Why Me? Why Not You? 5
I'm Still Learning 6
Yesterday 8
If You Stop By, Lord 9
God, Is My Father 11
I Have A Friend 13
Lord, Do It 15
There Was A Day 17
It's Some People Out There, Lord 19
When I Get Up 21
When God Calls 23
Time To Make A Decision 25
A Single Mom 27
My Family Life 29
My Coming Out Season 31
I Tried Some Things 33
Ayden's Day 35
My Psalms 23 38
My Special Cousin 40
Sometimes I Don't Know What To Say 42
My Big Family 45
Struggles Are Real 47
The Death of A Good Man 50
Your Story 52
Life Is Real 55
Thank God For Change 58

The Life of A Real Woman, Real But Healed

It's 5:25 a.m.	60
What Is A Friend?	63
Divorced Twice	66
The Doors of Faith	69
Are You Pregnant Too?	71
Called Out	73
H.S. (High School)	75
Singing Comforts Me	77
A Good Man	79
Love Me For Me	80
I Could Have	81
Knock At The Door	84
Two Angels, One On The Way	86
I Was Born Straight	88
Take Time	90
This is It	92
Love You, My Brother	94
"Are You Tired, Yet?"	97
A Book in Her	99
The End	102
I Didn't Want To Know	105
Holiday Inn	108
55, It's Time	111
I'm Free Now	114
"He's My Everything Now"	117
Crazy Faith	122
Holler or Yell	124
The Thief	127
All Messed Up	130
Word of Life	132
Baby Jordan	135

Singleness	137
The Baby of Five	140
Anxiety	143
Gout, But Got To Go	145
The Closet	147
The Power of Forgiveness	150
Revenge	152
Surprise	154
About the Author	156

A Quick Look

Let's take a quick look,
Before you turn the next page of this book.
God's intentions for me was to keep it real.
So, when you read it you could feel.

He asked me to lay it all out,
That's what this book is all about.
I wrote the way He gave it to me.
So, don't judge certain words you read.

If certain words offend you,
Talk to the Master; how things happened is true.
I struggled with some of the words,
But remember real, but healed, is what I heard.

I don't know no other way to be,
I guess that's why I'm free.

I didn't hide anything so God can trust me again.
I wanted to blot some things out,
But then your soul wouldn't rise and shout.

I put all of my laundry out there,
As long as you get free,
I really don't care!

People going to talk whether it's truth or a lie.
Destiny is on my life, don't have time to cry.
So I'm ready for the backlash.
It's about souls, not cash.

I was bold before I got saved.
I'm glad my past is in the grave.
I'm not worried about what carnal minds may think.
Show me somebody with a past that doesn't stink.

The Life of A Real Woman, Real But Healed

Thought I would give you a quick look,
So, you won't be surprised when you read the book.

So, brace your mind and your heart.
Get ready to turn the page and start.
Are you on your mark?

When you get to the end,
And it blesses you within;
Thank you for buying one for your friend.
Turn the page now and begin.

Just When You Think

Just when you think you know God, you really don't.
Just when you think it's over, it's just beginning.

Just when you think you're delivered, here "it" comes again.
Just when you think you're out of darkness, here comes more darkness.

Just when you think you're over this and that, here comes this and that.
Just when you think your bills are under control, here comes another one.

Just when you think you got God figured out, He comes another way.
Just when you think you know your sisters and brothers, here comes trouble.

Just when you think you heard God's voice, here comes the other choice.
Just when you think you're the head, here comes "tail".

Just when you think you're a lender, here comes the borrow.
Just when you think your faith is high, here comes low.

Just when you think it's settled, here comes disruption.
Just when you think you're healed, here comes pain.

Just when you think I know, here comes not sure.
Just when you think I got this, here comes let go.

Well, well, well!
In the midst of, "You think," Jesus knows.
In the midst of, "You think," Jesus cares.
In the midst of, "You think," Jesus will.
In the midst of, "You think," Jesus is able.
In the midst of, "You think," He's capable.
In the midst of, "You think," Jesus already thought about it.
In the midst of, "You think," it's already done.
So, stop thinking because Jesus knows.

The Reason

The reason I praise You is because You deserve it.
The reason why I worship You is because You're my God.

The reason why I submit to You is because You're my Husband.
The reason why You're my God is because there is no other.

The reason why I talk about You is because You're the Gospel.
The reason why I tell others about You is because You're my brother.

The reason why I serve You is because You're my guest of honor.
The reason why I live for You is because my old life was no good.

The reason why I'm saved is because You're my Savior.
The reason why I come through the doors of faith,
Is because I know what it takes.

The reason why You chose me is because I'm Your remnant.
The reason why I'm fearfully and wonderfully made,
Is because You started from the crown of my head.

The reason why I'm no longer a prostitute is because You bought me.
The reason why I love You is because You first loved me.

The reason why I'm holy is because You cleansed me.
The reason why I'm Yours is because I know You're mine.

The reason why I'm blessed is because You're my bless-er.
I don't really need a reason.
Do you?

We often times wonder why me? Why this happens to me? Why that happens to me? Why was I chosen for this and why not her? Why not Him? But sometimes can you just imagine Jesus saying, "Why not you?" *

Why Me? Why Not You?

I've been divorced twice. Why not you?
I've been broken-hearted. Why not you?
I've been lied on. Why not you?
I've been over-looked. Why not you?
I've been used. Why not you?
I've been last. Why not you?
I've been forgotten. Why not you?
I've been rejected. Why not you?
I've been persecuted. Why not you?
I've been talked about. Why not you?
I've been scorned. Why not you?
I've been through. Why not you?
I've been shunned. Why not you?
I'm saved now. Why not you?
I'm washed now. Why not you?
I'm healed now. Why not you?
I've been forgiven. Why not you?
I've been changed. Why not you?
I've been redeemed. Why not you?

I've been molded. Why not you?
I've been "set" free. Why not you?
Jesus did it for me. Why not you?
I'm no longer a victim. Why are you?

*Often times we can become frustrated in our relationship with God the Father, God the Son, God the Holy Spirit, and others we love simply because we fail to understand that we're all still learning. Learning is a process but God is a great Teacher. *

I'm Still Learning

I'm still learning how to treat Him.
I'm still learning how to greet Him.
I'm still learning how to believe Him.
I'm still learning how to receive Him.

I'm still learning how to wait.
I'm still learning how not to fake.
I'm still learning how to talk to Him.
I'm still learning how to walk with Him.

I'm still learning how to seek Him.
I'm still learning how to meet Him.
I'm still learning how to live.
I'm still learning how to give.

I'm still learning it's about Him.
I'm still learning it's in the Spiritual realm.
I'm still learning we are one.
I'm still learning it's already done.

I'm still learning He's my Father.
I'm still learning I'm not a bother.
I'm still learning, and it will never end.
I'm still learning He's my friend.

I'm still learning to pass the test.
I'm still learning how to rest.
I'm still learning, what about you?
I'm still learning what to do.

Carol Godfrey

I'm still learning to lay my life down.
I'm still learning how to get a crown.
I'm still learning life is worth living.
I'm still learning He's so giving.

I'm still learning how much He loves me.
I'm still learning His love is free.
I'm still learning I don't know it all.
I'm still learning how to get up from a fall.

I may not learn as fast as you.
Just be patient, God will see me through.
So through your understanding, teach others.
And remember He's the teacher like no other.

Yesterday

Yesterday has come and gone,
So let go and move on.

Yesterday is no longer here,
Live in God, and don't fear.

Yesterday is a day of the past,
Rejoice today and be glad.

Yesterday has nothing to do with today,
Keep moving, God will make a way.

Yesterday troubles and yesterday pains,
Are not today's future gains.

So step out of yesterday,
And live for today.

Today is all you have,
Rejoice in the Lord, don't be sad.

Today is a gift, chose to make that shift.
Don't know how, ask God for a lift.

Let Him lift you from yesterday,
Because He's already in today.

If You Stop By, Lord

If You stop by, Lord, I'll follow You.
If You stop by, Lord, I'll know what to do.

If You stop by, Lord, things are kind of tight.
If You stop by, Lord, I know it'll be alright.

If You stop by, Lord, I'll be healed.
If You stop by, Lord, It won't matter how I feel.

If You stop by, Lord, I won't be lonely.
If You stop by, Lord, I'll be your one and only.

If You stop by, Lord, on today,
If You stop by, Lord, I'll know the way.

If You stop by, Lord, I'll appreciate.
If You stop by, Lord, I won't hesitate.

If You stop by, Lord, I won't fear.
If You stop by, Lord, I'll come near.

If You stop by, Lord, I'll bow to You.
If You stop by, Lord, I'll be true.

If You stop by, Lord, I'll forsake all others.
If You stop by, Lord, there won't be another brother.

If You stop by, Lord, I won't leave my house.
If You stop by, Lord, I'll be quiet as a mouse.

If You stop by, Lord, I'll give You a hug.
If You stop by, Lord, I'll lay prostrate on the rug.

If You stop by, Lord, I'll give you a kiss.
If You stop by, Lord, I promise I won't miss.

The Life of A Real Woman, Real But Healed

If You stop by, Lord, I'll let you speak.
If You stop by, Lord, I'll be meek.

If You stop by, Lord, I'll welcome you in.
If You stop by, Lord, I'll confess all my sins.

If You stop by, Lord, you don't have to stay long.
If You stop by, Lord, I'll sing you a sweet song.

If You stop by, Lord, It won't take long.
If You stop by, Lord, you will soon find out.
This is where you belong.

God, Is My Father

God, is my Father, this I know.
God, is my Father, I have His DNA to prove it so.

God, is my Father, didn't have to go to court.
God, is my Father, my sins He did abort.

God, is my Father, look in my eyes.
God, is my Father, and you'll see thine.

God, is my Father, look at my walk.
God, is my Father, don't go by my talk.

God, is my Father, I have no doubt.
God, is my Father, because I'm never without.

God, is my Father, because when I call.
God, is my Father, He's never too busy at all.

God, is my Father, because He's always fair.
God, is my Father, because He always cares.

God, is my Father, because he went to Calvary.
God, is my Father, because He did it just for me.

God, is my Father, and I am His.
God, is my Father, He's my best friend.

God, is my Father, and wants to be yours.
God, is my Father, just open the door.

God, is my Father, His love is real.
God, is my Father, don't you want to feel?

God, is my Father, I have other sisters too.
God, is my Father, Sally, Rhonda, and Melinda just to name a few.

The Life of A Real Woman, Real But Healed

God, is my Father, because I'm the baby of them all.
God, is my Father, ask Clarence, Phyllis, and Charles.

God, is my Father, ask my Mother.
God, is my Father, she'll tell you there's no other.

God, is my Father, and He's the best.
God, is my Father, I took the blood test.

God, is my Father, the results are in.
God, is my Father, I know because he lives within.

In case you were wondering who my Father was,
Go tell everybody He's the God above.

I Have A Friend

I have a friend I'll like to introduce you to.
He's a wonderful friend and Counselor too.

I have a friend who's a friend of mine.
He'll be your friend, you don't need a dime.

I have a friend when you're in trouble or in need.
Call him, He's a friend indeed.

I have a friend when nights are cold.
Call the Comforter, so I've been told.

I have a friend who will never leave you.
I have a friend that will see you through.

I have a friend who has a big heart.
I have a friend that gives brand new starts.

I have a friend I call all the time.
I have a friend who brings peace-be-thine.

I have a friend who is faithful and true.
I have a friend, "Thank you, Jesus, it's You."

I have a friend who saved my soul.
I have a friend who made me whole.

I have a friend who took my mess.
I have a friend who gave me His best.

I have a friend who taught me how to love.
I have a friend that sent it from above.

I have a friend name Rhonda Lynn.
I have a spiritual friend name Beginning and End.

I have a friend I try to obey.
I have a friend who is the Way.

I have a friend, will you accept Him today?
I have a friend, please don't push Him away.
I have a friend who will never leave but stay.

Lord, Do It

Lord, do it, like only you can.
Lord, do it, with your mighty hand.

Lord, do it, you have the power.
Lord, do it, even if she's in the shower.

Lord, do it, my daughter need you.
Lord, do it, I believe in you too.

Lord, do it, she has gone astray.
Lord, do it, shape her Your way.

Lord, do it, she's my only one.
Lord, do it, through Your Son.

Lord, do it, her Daddy left her alone.
Lord, do it, before you call Him home.

Lord, do it, she has three on her own.
Lord, do it, even though I know it was wrong.

Lord, do it, if only for me.
Lord, do it, set my daughter free.

Lord, do it, her Mother has the faith.
Lord, do it, please don't hesitate.

Lord, do it, before I die.
Lord, do it, I'll be sure to testify.

Lord, do it, she's a pretty good girl.
Lord, do it, but not through the world.

Lord, do it, for Ayden and Samiyah.
Lord, do it, because you're Jehovah-Jireh.

Lord, do it, sometimes, times get hard.
Lord, do it, Because you're our "Star."

Lord, do it, for my family.
Lord, do it, like you done for John and Mary.

Lord, do it, I'll be grateful and true.
Lord, do it, just for you.

Lord, do it, some family need you today.
Lord, do it, they really needed you yesterday.

To the family who need God to do it.
Worship and praise God on through it.

There Was A Day

There was a day, my life was out of control.
That was the day, the devil had me on hold.

There was a day, I tried some pot.
That was the day, my breath was shot.

There was a day, I was supposed to give birth.
That was the day, my heart was hurt.

There was a day, I was the talk of the town.
That was the day, my life turned around.

There was a day, I wanted to walk away.
That was the day, Jesus asked me to stay.

There was a day, I couldn't stand on my two feet.
That was the day, I couldn't make ends meet.

There was a day, I lost my home.
That was the day, I didn't feel so grown.

There was a day, I had a business of my own.
That was the day, looked up it was gone.

There was a day, the husband was gone.
That was the day, I was alone.

There was a day, I had no car.
That was the day, I couldn't get far.

There was a day, I had no funds.
That was the day, I wanted to run.

There was a day, they picked up my truck.
That was the day, I was stuck.

The Life of A Real Woman, Real But Healed

There was a day, my friends left me.
That was the day, God said get on your knees.

There was a day, depression found me.
That was the day, I was no longer free.

There was a day, I was called to faith.
That was a day, I had to take.

There was a day, I walked to work.
That was the day, my feet hurt.

There was a day, it was dark and dreary.
That was the day, my eyes were teary.

There was a day, my heart was bleeding.
That was the day, I had to start kneeling.

There was a day, I had no more fight.
That was the day, Jesus made it right.

Are you having one of these days?
Lift your voice and say,
Jesus, I need your grace.

The power is in your tongue, speak it now.
Put the devil on the run.

All it takes is faith.
Now enjoy your day,
That the Lord made.

It's Some People Out There, Lord

It's some people out there, Lord, who need your grace.
It's some people out there, Lord, who need to see your face.

It's some people out there, Lord, all alone.
It's some people out there, Lord, can't find their way back home.

It's some people out there, Lord, body full of cancer.
It's some people out there, Lord, who need to know You paid the ransom.

It's some people out there, Lord, on drugs and alcohol.
It's some people out there, Lord, who need to know You paid it all.

It's some people out there, Lord, who need to be saved.
It's some people out there, Lord, I know You can raise.

It's some people out there, Lord, who don't want to be on the street.
It's some people out there, Lord, I wish You could meet.

It's some people out there, Lord, in jail.
It's some people out there, Lord, can't make bail.

It's some people out there, Lord, all they wanted was to be loved.
It's some people out there, Lord, I wish You would hug.

It's some people out there, Lord, who are depressed.
It's some people out there, Lord, who can't rest.

It's some people out there, Lord, shooting drugs in their veins.
It's some people out there, Lord, who don't know, You reign.

It's some people out there, Lord, thinking about taking their life.
It's some people out there, Lord,
Don't know You're the Way, the Truth, and the Life.

The Life of A Real Woman, Real But Healed

It's some people out there, Lord, who didn't commit the crime.
It's some people out there, Lord, just need a moment of Your time.

It's some people out there, Lord, who left the church.
It's some people out there, Lord, because they got hurt.

It's some people out there, Lord, I can't reach.
It's some people out there, Lord, I hope You'll teach.

It's some people out there, Lord, looking for grace.
It's some people out there, Lord, all they need is a taste.

It's some people out there, Lord, who need Your mercy.
It's some people out there, Lord, who need it in a hurry.

It's some people out there, Lord, Just need a lift.
It's some people out there, Lord, I need You to shift.

It's some people out there, Lord, who are at the end.
It's some people out there, Lord, just need you to be a friend.

There's someone out there, Lord, who need to know my God.
There's someone out there, Lord, life for them is hard.

If you're that someone out there today,
Keep looking up, God will make a way.

When I Get Up

When I get up, it's just you and me.
When I get up, I say, "Thank thee."

When I get up, I sit on the side of the bed.
When I get up, I lift my head.

When I get up, I take a leak.
When I get up, the Son is speaking.

When I get up, I start to pray.
When I get up, I say, "Lord, You lead the way."

When I get up, it's about 6:00 a.m.
When I get up, I'm looking for the "I Am."

When I get up, the tears begin to fall.
When I get up, and realize He's the greatest of them all.

When I get up, I repent of my sins.
When I get up, I need to be cleansed.

When I get up, I let the Holy Spirit have His way.
When I get up, I'm ready for the day.

When I get up, I open my heart.
When I get up, I don't want to part.

When I get up, sometimes I'm a little slow.
When I get up, the Spirit says, "Let's go."

When I get up, I hear the pots and pans.
When I get up, Carol, just take a stand.

The Life of A Real Woman, Real But Healed

When I get up, I see three gifts from above.
When I get up, they show me so much love.

When I get up, it's a full day.
When I get up, it's faith all the way.

When I get up, it's all about Him.
When I get up, it's not about them.

When I get up, I want the love of God.
When I get up, that's sometimes hard.

When I get up, I want to do my best.
When I get up, "Lord, you do the rest."

When I get up, I need a word from the Lord.
When I get up, because I know it won't come back void.

When I get up, I want to feel His embrace.
When I get up, "Lord, I want to do it your way."

When I get up, "Satan, you're going down."
When I get up, I don't have time to be bound.

When I get up, I shout VICTORY.
When I get up, I tell Satan, "Get behind thee."

So, when you get up in the morning, try these things:

When you get up, watch Jesus reign.
When you get up, call His name.
When you get up, watch your day change.

When God Calls

When God calls, what do you say?
When God calls , do you say, "Not today?"

When God calls, can you hear?
When God calls, do you fear?

When God calls, do you ignore?
When God calls, do you open the door?

When God calls, do you think it's Sam?
When God calls, do you know it's the "I Am?"

When God calls, His voice is like no other.
When God calls, don't mistake Him for your brother.

When God calls, don't ignore the ring.
When God calls, you don't want to miss a thing.

When God calls, there's no 3-way.
When God calls, it's His way.

When God calls, don't send Him to voicemail.
When God calls, say, "I'll be right there."

When God calls, don't say, "I have someone on the line."
When God calls, you better give Him some time.

When God calls, don't have an attitude.
When God calls, don't say, "What's up dude?"

When God calls, it's not a prank.
When God calls, if I was you, I'll take rank.

When God calls, open your heart.
When God calls, He wants to give you a new start.

The Life of A Real Woman, Real But Healed

When God calls, He's not wasting time.
When God calls, He has a purpose in mind.

When God calls, be sweet and kind.
When God calls, ask Him, "What's on your mind?"

When God calls, don't say, "What you want now?"
When God calls, say, "Wow!"

When God calls, tell Him your troubles.
When God calls, don't you murmur.

When God calls, don't you complain.
When God calls, ask Him to reign.

When God calls, don't say hold on.
When God calls, answer the phone.

When God calls, you might be at the mall.
When God calls, you may be in the hall.

So the next time He calls, don't mistake Him for Paul.

Time To Make A Decision

Time to make a decision. Who will it be?
Will it be mother, brother, or auntie?
Time to make a decision. Who will it be?
Will it be love or jealousy?

Time to make a decision. Who will it be?
Your daughter or your son.
Time to make a decision. Who will it be?
Because they are on the run.

Time to make a decision. Who will it be?
Will it be Charles or Will-ie?
Time to make a decision. Who will it be?
Will it be bound or will it be free?

Time to make a decision. Who will it be?
Will it be suicide or defeat?
Time to make a decision. Who will it be?
Rise up, God gave you the victory.

Time to make a decision. Who will it be?
Will it be slavery or will it be sin?
Time to make a decision. Who will it be?
Will it be salvation and mercy?

Time to make a decision. Who will it be?
Will it be sex or porn?
Time to make a decision. Who will it be?
Will it be Christ and be reborn?

Time to make a decision. Who will it be?
Will it be Sha-nae or Sallie?
Time to make a decision. Who will it be?
Will it be grace and mercy?

Time to make a decision. Who will it be?
Will it be needles and drugs?
Time to make a decision. Who will it be?
Will it be Jesus and His love?

Time to make a decision. Who will it be?
Will it be Satan, the liar, and the thief?
Time to make a decision. Who will it be?
Will it be Jesus, and Calvary?

Time to make a decision. Who will it be?
Will it be the lottery or money?
Time to make a decision. Who will it be?
Will it be my Savior who gave His life for thee?

Time to make a decision. One you won't regret.
Time to make a decision. One I know you won't forget.

Time to make a decision. What will it be?
Time to make a decision. Hell or eternity.

Time to make a decision. Bound or free.
Time to make a decision. Will it be Jesus, the Almighty?

If you're not sure of the choice,
Just listen to the still small voice.

A Single Mom

Are you, A Single Mom, looking for love?
A Single Mom, just needing a hug?

A Single Mom, feeling like you can't cope?
A Single Mom, Who has lost hope?

A Single Mom, with one child and three grands?
A Single Mom, needing the Lord's hand?

A Single Mom, with tears in her eyes.
A Single Mom, needing the Son to shine?

A Single Mom, tired of child support court?
A Single Mom, trying to hold down the fort?

A Single Mom, with a place she can't afford?
A Single Mom, times are just hard.

A Single Mom, on welfare cheese?
A Single Mom, found herself in need?

A Single Mom, who's hardly at home?
A Single Mom, with a child feeling alone?

A Single Mom, pulling two shifts?
A Single Mom, needing a lift?

A single Mom, lights about to be cut out?
A Single Mom, looking for a way out?

A Single Mom, going through a series of test?
A Single Mom, "Lord, just needing some rest."

A Single Mom, looking for a break-thru?
A Single Mom, just don't know what to do.

A Single Mom, waiting on the Lord.
A single Mom, trying to serve.

A Single Mom, sold out!
A Single Mom, trying to hold out!

A Single Mom, the struggle is real.
A Single Mom, needing to be healed.

A Single Mom, needing the master's touch.
A Single Mom, who don't have much.

A Single Mom, on God's waiting list.
A single Mom, waiting to hear, "This is it!"

To my single moms, you're not alone.
To my single moms, be strong!

To my single moms, pray and wait!
To my single moms, God will send you a mate.

My Family Life

I was born a Godfrey.
My mother was a Bail-ey.

My family life was sometimes hard.
Even when I tried to do my part.

My family had its ups and downs.
But Jesus turned it around.

I have a sister and two brothers.
I would say they're like no others.

I have a Mother name Edna Mae.
She's a giver and not a take.

I'm the baby of five.
My brother Dennis he died.

My father Albert was a carpenter.
Just like Joseph, Mary's partner.

I have a daughter C.C. for short.
I have a child like Mary; I'm glad I didn't abort.

I have two grands, and one on the way.
Praying, none of them, will go astray.

My family is rather tight.
Even though we have our fights.

My family is no different than yours.
Sometimes their thoughts are all out doors.

My family didn't have a fancy car.
But had one and got far.

The Life of A Real Woman, Real But Healed

My family house wasn't like others.
But it covered my sister and my brothers.

My father and mother were strict.
It was obey or the stick.

I ran away from home one day.
I went to Newland, Donna house to stay.

I was tired of Godfrey's rules.
So, I packed my bags and skipped school.

My family didn't try to be like next door.
Even though, it seems like they had more.

They could go out and play out doors.
Seems like we always had chores.

I remember Dennis and Dad had a fight.
But before they passed, through Christ, they made it right.

After Christ, all you have is family.
Don't be the one they don't see.

Family will be there when friends leave.
Go through a struggle and ya'll see.

God ordained family,
Ask John and Mary.

Pick up that strife and jealousy.
So family can be free.

Why don't you pick up your phone, text, or tweet?
Tell that brother, sister, or auntie I forgive thee.

Because we're family.

My Coming Out Season

Are you tired of being in the dump?
Tell depression go and get off your hump.

We all go through seasons of fair,
Wondering if anybody care.

We all go through seasons of fear,
Wondering, "God are you near?"

We all go through seasons of will this end?
Needing Jesus to step in as a friend.

We all go through seasons of is it my time?
Should I do this or wait on thine?

We all go through seasons of will I succeed or fail?
Ask God, He will tell.

We all go through seasons of being alone.
Even if the husband and wife are home.

We all go through seasons of being overwhelmed.
And can't find the right person to tell.

We all go through seasons of I need a break.
But when you see the funds, it says, can't take.

We all go through a season of I can't do this anymore.
Then you look, God has open a door.

We all go through seasons of wanting to quit.
Only to hear Him say, "That's not it."

We all go through seasons of sickness and pain.
That's how we found out Jesus reigns.

We all go through seasons of unbelief,
Instead of praying for belief.

We all go through seasons of sorrow,
Because we forget Jesus holds tomorrow.

We all go through seasons of when am I coming out?
When we learn to open our mouth and shout.

When am I coming out?
When we learn to worship and not doubt.

When am I coming out?
When we speak the word out of our mouth.

When am I coming out?
When we tell fear, "Get out my house!"

When am I coming out?
When we learn to shout and not pout.

When am I coming out?
When we learn it's not about me.

I can't tell you when.
All I can tell you is, you're gonna win.

It's your coming out season,
March on through.
I just told you what to do!

There's an "In season and Out of season," too.
Shout in and shout out, too!
Prophetess Carol is rooting for you.

Ecclesiastes 3, "To everything there is a season."
It won't be long.
Stay strong!
Your season will come.

I Tried Some Things

I tried some things, of the world.
I tried some things, I'm not proud of.

I tried some things, before I got saved.
I tried some things, before I knew Jesus name.

I tried some things, I thought I was big enough to do.
I tried some things, I was told not to.

I tried some things, with Deon, Travis, and Tony.
I tried some things, and thought it was funny.

I tried some things, could have cost me my life.
I tried some things, I know wasn't right.

I tried some things, I thought was cool.
I tried some things, because it was my bedroom.

I tried some things, just to fit in.
I tried some things, I won't try again.

I tried some things, I would never tell.
I tried some things, could have sent me to Hell.

I tried some things, could have cost me my mind.
I tried some things, didn't cost me a dime.

I tried some things, both great and small.
I tried some things, can't tell it all.

I tried some things, became the talk of the town.
I tried some things, that made me frown.

I tried some things, like getting drunk.
I tried some things, I'll like to bump.

The Life of A Real Woman, Real But Healed

I tried some things, like smoking marijuana.
I tried some things, didn't cost me no money.

I tried some things, stealing for one.
I tried some things, that was just dumb.

I tried some things, like cussing people out.
I tried some things, without a doubt.

I tried some things, that came back to me.
I tried some things, that wasn't on Calvary.

I tried some things, that's now on the cross.
I tried some things, I'm glad you're not the boss.

I tried some things, Satan still tries to remind me.
I tried some things, I remind him, get behind thee!

I tried some things, what about you?
I tried some things, people don't have a clue.

I tried some things, I regret.
I tried some things, I wish to forget.

I tried some things, but I'm free now.
I tried some things, because I was a clown.

I tried some things, before I found Christ.
I tried some things, now my future is bright.

Now those things you're not proud of, give it to Christ who sits above.
And when the enemy tries to remind you of those things,
Remind him that Eternal Life I've gained.

And when people try to remind you of what you used to do,
Ask them, "What about you?"
Don't let people dwell on your past.
Tell them it's in the graveyard; it passed.

Ayden's Day

There was a day while I was at work.
It was a day my heart hurt.

It was a day filled with pain.
It was a day wondering if God would reign.

It was a day tears flowed from my eyes.
It was a day I couldn't hide.

It was a day darkness was all-around.
It was a day I didn't want to be found.

It was a day I wanted to just stay in the house.
It was a day I could hardly move about.

It was a day that felt like death.
It was a day I had nothing left.

It was a day I'll call Ayden's Day.
It was a day Satan wanted his way.

It was a day I had to leave work early.
It was a day no more hair curling.

It was a day I was separated from my grandson.
It was a day I was done.

It was a day he was only about four months.
It was a day all I could do was grunt.

It was a day I thought my daughter would lose her mind.
It was a day the sun wasn't shining.

It was a day I'll call Ayden's Day.
It was a day Grand-ma had to pray.

The Life of A Real Woman, Real But Healed

It was a day Samiyah was alone.
It was a day she asked, "When bro coming home?"

It was a day Sierra couldn't sleep.
It was a day neither could we.

It was a day she was in and out the house.
It was a day I couldn't tell everybody about.

It was a day I thought would never end.
It was a day I found out who were my friends.

It was a day they say she left him on the steps.
It was a day I needed God's help.

It was a day I said, "No way!"
It was a day he stayed.

It was a day we didn't know the law.
It was a day we had to make a call.

It was a day she didn't have a dime.
It was a day I had to give up mine.

It was a day it was me, Sally, and Mom.
It was a day Satan had caused harm.

It was a day Prophet Perkins said, "Restitution."
It was a day the prophecy was true.

It was a day the verdict was in.
It was a day Judge Jesus put it to an end.

It was a day, it was Ayden's Day.
It was a day God was going to have His way.

It was Ayden's Day the decision was in.
It was Ayden's Day he was home again.

Carol Godfrey

It was Ayden's Day we went to pick him up.
It was Ayden's Day we couldn't hug enough.

It was Ayden's Day when we got home.
It was Ayden's Day all he wanted to do was roam.

It was Ayden's Day didn't want him out of our sight.
It was Ayden's Day and his future is bright.

Mothers and Fathers be careful what you do.
Because your children are counting on you.

So if you're going through an Ayden's Day.
Lift your voice and say, "God, have Your way!"

My Psalms 23

My Psalms 23, is about Dad, Mom, and me.
My Psalms 23, started in 1963.

My Psalms 23, started when Dad and Mom decided to have me.
My Psalms 23, I was the last one in thee.

My Psalms 23, I was their baby girl.
My Psalms 23, I was their gift to the world.

My Psalms 23, I was their pride and joy.
My Psalms 23, it was when they said no more.

My Psalms 23, I had both of my parents.
My Psalms 23, sometimes I took them for granted.

My Psalms 23, included my sister and brothers.
My Psalms 23, didn't include others.

My Psalms 23, is my daughter's birthday.
My Psalms 23, I told Dr. Kizen no way.

My Psalms 23, is a grandbaby day.
My Psalms 23, Baby Miyah came this way.

My Psalms 23, was how long I did hair.
My Psalms 23, was when God asked me to walk away.

My Psalms 23, I told Mom what God said.
My Psalms 23, she said obey and be glad.

My Psalms 23, has been a journey.
My Psalms 23, didn't come with a honey.

My Psalms 23, I had to trust God.
My Psalms 23, it was sometimes hard.

Carol Godfrey

My Psalms 23, He was with me all the way.
My Psalms 23, He made my day.

My Psalms 23, we have truly been blessed.
My Psalms 23, even though there are days I miss Daddy.

My Psalms 23, has a lot of family memories.
My Psalms 23, has another missing from the tree.

My Psalms 23, included a jack of all trades.
My Psalms 23, is now resting in his grave.

My Psalms 23, included my brother, Dennis G.
My Psalms 23, God set him free.

My Psalms 23, may be without two.
My Psalms 23, still got a strong few.

My Psalms 23, still got love and joy.
My Psalms 23, got peace, grace, and so much more.

My Special Cousin

a.k.a. June Bug

My special cousin, God set him free.
My special cousin, went before me.

My special cousin, he was like no other.
My special cousin, was like a brother.

My special cousin, he was my age.
My special cousin, he was great.

My special cousin, had a contagious laugh.
My special cousin, would give you his last.

My special cousin, he was a good man.
My special cousin, was my friend.

My special cousin, loved hotdogs.
My special cousin, liked them great and small.

My special cousin, he could not talk.
My special cousin, use to couldn't walk.

My special cousin, had two sisters he loved.
My special cousin, had Sharon, Nita, and God above.

My special cousin, loved the Dallas Cowboys.
My special cousin, when they won it was noise.

My special cousin, had the hat, coat, and shoes.
My special cousin, wouldn't wear them when they lose.

My special cousin, never complained.
My special cousin, went through a lot of pain.

Carol Godfrey

My special cousin, was God's gift from above.
My special cousin, never felt my last hug.

My special cousin, had a peace on His face.
My special cousin, had run his race.

My special cousin, was born April 17th, 1964.
My special cousin, will be inside Heaven's door.

My special cousin, passed away on October 23rd.
My special cousin, never heard me speak another word.

My special cousin, this is for you.
My special cousin, we, the Godfrey family, love and miss you too.

My special cousin, we're okay.
My special cousin, we have our days.

My special cousin, thank you for your light.
My special cousin, you taught me how to fight.

Thank you, Uncle Frank, and Aunt Lois.
Thank you for sharing your boy.

If you have a special child rise up and be proud.

Thank you, Sharon, and Nita, our family loves thee.
So when October 23rd comes around look towards Heaven and see Thee.

Sometimes I Don't Know What To Say

Sometimes I don't know what to say,
About this Jesus who saves my day.
Sometimes I don't know what to say,
About my Jesus who makes a way.

Sometimes I don't know what to say,
About my Jesus whom I adore.
Sometimes I don't know what to say,
About my Jesus who opened this door.

Sometimes I don't know what to say,
About my Jesus who gives me the victory.
Sometimes I don't know what to say,
About Him who helps me to see.

Sometimes I don't know what to say,
About my Jesus who wakes me up.
Sometimes I don't know what to say,
About my Jesus who was so tough.

Sometimes I don't know what to say,
About my Jesus who gives me grace.
Sometimes I don't know what to say,
About my Jesus who helps me run this race.

Sometimes I don't know what to say,
About my Jesus who calms my storms.
Sometimes I don't know what to say,
About my Jesus who keeps me from harm.

Sometimes I don't know what to say,
About my Jesus who took this pen.
Sometimes I don't know what to say,
About my Jesus who said write what's within.

Carol Godfrey

Sometimes I don't know what to say,
About my Jesus who kept me out of jail.
Sometimes I don't know what to say,
About my Jesus who pulled me from Hell.

Sometimes I don't know what to say,
About my Jesus who forgave me.
Sometimes I don't know what to say,
About my Jesus who raised thee.

Sometimes I don't know what to say,
About my Jesus who loves me.
Sometimes I don't know what to say,
About my Jesus who died on the cross for thee.

Sometimes I don't know what to say,
About my Jesus who keeps me.
Sometimes I don't know what to say,
About my Jesus who treats thee.

Sometimes I don't know what to say,
About my Jesus who pays my bills.
Sometimes I don't know what to say,
About my Jesus who loves to give.

Sometimes I don't know what to say,
About my Jesus who heals me.
Sometimes I don't know what to say,
About my Jesus who feels me.

Sometimes I don't know what to say,
About my Jesus who is so sweet.
Sometimes I don't know what to say,
About my Jesus who is so neat.

Sometimes I don't know what to say,
About my Jesus who is true.
Sometimes I don't know what to say,
About my Jesus who makes all things new.

The Life of A Real Woman, Real But Healed

Sometimes I don't know what to say,
About my Jesus who gave me a chance.
Sometimes I don't know what to say,
About my Jesus who took another glance.

Sometimes I don't know what to say,
About my Jesus who never leaves me alone.
Sometimes I don't know what to say,
About my Jesus who visits my home.

Sometimes I don't know what to say,
About my Jesus who gave me Himself, the Son.
Sometimes I don't know what to say,
About my Jesus who didn't run.

Sometimes I don't know what to say,
About my Jesus who don't lie.
Sometimes I don't know what to say,
About my Jesus who wipes my eyes.

Sometimes I don't know what to say,
About my Jesus who gave me a right to the Tree of Life.
Sometimes I don't know what to say,
About my Jesus who knows I'm not right.

Sometimes I don't know what to say,
About my Jesus, the man I love.
Sometimes I don't know what to say,
About my Jesus who ascended like a dove.

Sometimes I don't know what to say,
About my Jesus who sleeps with me at night.
Sometimes I don't know what to say,
About my Jesus who holds me tight.

Sometimes I don't know what to say,
To a God that's so great.
Sometimes I don't know what to say,
So I think I'll close and say, "Hey!"

My Big Family

I come from a big family,
On both sides of the tree.
The Bailey's and the Godfrey's,
Well known in E.C.

When I would walk down the street,
Some would say, "Are you a Godfrey?"
Sometimes I wondered if I would,
Have my own identity.

Some would say, "Who's your Mother?"
Then they'll say, "Is Bill her brother?"
Then they'd want to know, "Who's your Father?"
I'll tell them his name is Albert.

Is that the man who does carpentry?
They'll say, "Oh yes, you're His."
I never doubted if he was mine.
All you have to do was look in my eyes.

My Mother only had that one man,
So I know I was the work of his hand.

My Dad was from Weeksville,
A place on the outskirts of town.
Where you needed a car to get around.

There were twelve of them in all.
They had broad shoulders and rather tall.

He was a hard-working man,
He made sure his family had.
It seemed small to others,
But not to me, my sister, and my brothers.

The Life of A Real Woman, Real But Healed

My Mother came from a family of thirteen.
Her parents stayed in the bed, so it seemed.
There were four boys and nine girls,
One passed away, so I heard.

There're two girls missing from the family.
Patricia Mae and Mary.
Henry and Ella Mae are also gone on.
So is the house the family owned.

I love them all; they're my family.
The Godfrey's and the Bailey's.
So whether your family is big or small,
God requires us to love them all.

Whether mixed, white or black,
Love of family is just right.
Love your family, hate the sin.
Call them up, say, let's meet again.

It doesn't matter who's right or who's wrong,
God intended family to be strong and to bond.
So drop the pride today,
Pick up that phone and tell your family, I love you anyway.

Because when they die it's too late.
Pick up that phone; don't hesitate.
Don't be the branch missing from the tree.
Just love your family.

Struggles Are Real

Don't let nobody lie to you; struggles are real.
They are the things you really feel.

Struggles come in all form, and they often cause us harm.
Struggles are real, sometimes I wondered if I would ever heal.

Don't let nobody lie to you; struggles are real.
Sometimes it can be getting out the bed.
Sometimes it can be as simple as lifting your head.

Don't let nobody lie to you; struggles are real.
Am I a boy, a girl, or both?
Struggles are real, if you don't know who you are, you won't get far.

Don't let nobody lie to you; struggles are real.
Talk to somebody who is true.

Don't let nobody lie to you; they haven't been good all their life.
Find somebody who got it right.

Struggles are real, ask Adam and Eve.
Struggles are real, Satan made Eve a deal.

Don't let nobody lie to you; struggles are real.
When lust tell you it's alright, but then salvation says, "Fight!"

Struggles are real, they cause guilt and shame.
But let me tell you the blood of Jesus can remove those names.

Don't let nobody lie to you; struggles are real.
They start in the heart, and their purpose is to pull you apart.

Struggles are real; it can be fantasies.
If you don't rebuke them then they become real.

The Life of A Real Woman, Real But Healed

Don't let nobody lie to you; struggles are real.
Some of them are really deep.
Struggles are real; and every now and then they try to creep.

Don't let nobody lie to you; struggles are real.
Ask depression!
Struggles are real, and so is oppression and recession.
Struggles are real, sometimes it can be our mouth.
Struggles are real, ask the spirit of doubt.

Don't let nobody lie to you; struggles are real.
It can be money, and friends think it's funny; struggles are real.
When you don't know how you gonna pay that loan,
And Creditors are calling you on the phone. Struggles are real.

Don't let nobody lie to you; struggles are real.
Abandonment is real.
Ask a child whose father left, and they aren't healed.

Don't let nobody lie to you; struggles are real.
Ask a mother who got no support from the father of her child.
Realizing he was just a sperm donor, and ran away and lied.

Don't let nobody lie to you; struggles are real.
Ask a mother trying to keep shoes, and clothes on their feet and backs.
Going to the store looking for something cheap off the rack.

Don't let nobody lie to you; struggles are real.
Ask a mother who worked day and night.
As a child, Mamma told them times were tight.

Don't let nobody lie to you; struggles are real.
Landlord want his rent.
Struggles are real, and you trying to make ends meet.

Struggles are real, then your child bring another
mouth in the house.
Struggles are real, and you want to ask her,
what were you thinking about?

Carol Godfrey

Don't let nobody lie to you, struggles are real.
Now you're on welfare.
Struggles are real, seems like nobody care.

Struggles are real, child needs lunch money.
Struggles are real, and you done have none.

Don't let nobody lie to you; struggles are real.
You trying to work and get called out to the school.
Struggles are real, because your child acting a fool.

Struggles are real, had to give up your place.
Struggles are real, at the moment you don't know grace.

Don't let nobody lie to you; struggles are real.
During this time, you didn't know God was real.
Struggles are real, I didn't know God could heal.

Struggles are real, didn't have a relationship with Christ like I do now.
Struggles are real, didn't know he was around.

Don't let nobody lie to you; struggles are real.
But you don't have to struggle alone.
Struggles are real, ask the prodigal son.

Struggles are real, seek the Lord and reach out to other saints.
Struggles are real, find some real sisters and learn the aint's.

Don't let nobody lie to you; struggles are real.
But they won't last always.
Struggles are real, I've been through now I can tell.

Struggles are real, you are not the only one.
Struggles are real, ask Jesus Christ, God's only begotten Son.

Don't let nobody lie to you; struggles are real.
Jesus went through and so will we.
Struggles are real, deal with them and be healed.

The Death of A Good Man

There was a day I had to move back home.
It wasn't my choice; all my money was gone.
I was living on Jones Avenue, it was my first home too.

I got behind in my mortgage.
Clients at work had become a shortage.
I had a move out date, had too much stuff to take.

I had to have a garage sale.
Remember now, I didn't have a male.
I had to move soon, and where I was going didn't have a lot of room.

It was hard to move back home, simply because I had been on my own.
I couldn't see God had a plan.
All I know was I wasn't glad.

My life was about to take a turn.
Didn't want to go back where I came from.

Had to ask Dad could I move back in.
Had to ask him because he was the man.
Not knowing God was unfolding his plan.

At this time, he could do for himself.
He didn't really need Mom, Clarence, or my help.
But then the day came it wasn't sunny, but rain.

Dad's health was failing right before my eyes,
I waited till I went to bed before I would cry.
I was trying to work and help out too.
After all he was my Dad that's what I was supposed to do.

Even though he was moody at times,
Don't matter, he was mine.

Carol Godfrey

He had his ways and so did I.
But I wasn't ready for him to die.

God brought me back home, so Mom wouldn't be alone.
He waited until we went to bed.
Mom was lying in the room didn't know he was dead.

Clarence got up to go to work.
That's the morning we were all hurt.
The death of a good man who had been the father of five,
Was no longer on this side.

The death of this good man born in 1934.
In 2011 God closed the door.
He left a good woman and five children behind.
That's okay, good man, peace be thine.

Your Story

People think they know your story;
But behind the story is God's glory.
People think they know you, when in reality, they have no clue.

People think they know you;
Because of your Mom and Dad, when in reality, family life was bad.

People think they know you;
Because of your skin, when in reality, who I am, is within.

People think they know you;
Because of your hair, when in reality, it could be bare.

People think they know you;
Because of your job, when in reality, my life was hard.

People think they know you;
Because of your money, when in reality,
You don't know how it's running.

People think they know you;
Because of the Journey you drive, when in reality,
They don't know if it's mine.

People think they know you;
Because of your clothes, when in reality,
They may have been stole.

People think they know you;
Because of what somebody else said, when in reality,
That issue is dead.

People think they know you;
Because of what Mama said, when in reality,
She spoke while mad.

Carol Godfrey

People think they know you;
Because of what Daddy said, when in reality,
He didn't finish his grade.

People think they know you;
So they talk to you any kind of way, when in reality,
They had a bad day.

People think they know you;
Because of what your co-workers said, when in reality,
They're trying to get a raise.

People think they know you;
Because of what your daughter said, when in reality,
She's just as bad.

People think they know you;
Because you walk like a boy, when in reality,
It was basketball the sport.

People think they know you;
Because you walk like a girl, when in reality,
You were touched by the world.

People think they know you;
Because others describe you, when in reality, it's not true.

People think they know you;
Because of what's not said, when in reality, I didn't go to bed.

People think they know you;
Because of the anointing on your life, when in reality,
They don't know the price.

People think they know you;
Because you can sing, when in reality, it's about the King.

People think they know you;
Because you're single, when in reality, you want to mingle.

The Life of A Real Woman, Real But Healed

People think they know you;
Because things look well, when reality is,
You're going through hell.

People think they know you;
Because the Spirit revealed, when in reality,
It was the purpose of being healed.

Don't be ashamed of your story.
Just know it's for God's glory.

Life Is Real

Life is real, but you can be healed.
Life is real, all you need to do is kneel.

Life is real, it is not a fantasy.
Life is real, open your eyes; you'll see.

Life is real, don't fall into Satan's traps.
Life is real, and so is his attack.

Life is real, it is no joke.
Life is real, it's more than a coke.

Life is real, ask Adam and Eve.
Life is real, the serpent came to steal.

Life is real, ask Joseph and Mary.
Life is real, I know, I had a baby.

Life is real, ask Jesus, the Son of God.
Life is real, it can be downright hard.

Life is real, it's not a fairy tale.
Life is real, it's Heaven or Hell.

Life is real, your name is all you got.
Life is real, it's tough when it get shot.

Life is real, loneliness is no joke.
Life is real, ask somebody who smokes.

Life is real, ask pain.
Life is real, when you're waiting on God to reign.

Life is real, the mortgage is due.
Life is real, and your baby need shoes.

The Life of A Real Woman, Real But Healed

Life is real, no child support.
Life is real, and you tired of court.

Life is real, been out of food.
Life is real, and all you can say is, I wish I could.

Life is real, Daddy not around.
Life is real, he acting like a clown.

Life is real, being called a "slut."
Life is real, it hurts.

Life is real, got somebody else's man.
Life is real, just because you can.

Life is real, smoke some dope.
Life is real, cause you lost hope.

Life is real, got your lights cut out.
Life is real, and your husband on the couch.

Life is real, and you want to die.
Life is real, and all you can do is cry.

Life is real, had to close your shop.
Life is real, don't let nobody tell you it's not.

Life is real, got your truck picked up.
Life is real, and now you're stuck.

Life is real, and you got to go back home.
Life is real, now you're not your own.

Life is real, you're in over draft.
Life is real, because you didn't do the math.

Life is real, bill collector's calling.
Life is real, you at the mall shopping.

Carol Godfrey

Life is real, go to jail.
Life is real, and need some bail.

Life is real, husband running around.
Life is real, you want to cut him up and down.

Life is real, the woman picking at you.
Life is real, you want to shoot her too.

Life is real, you doing the best you can.
Life is real, people don't understand.

Life is real, and so are you.
Life is real, trust God and be true.

Thank God For Change

Thank God for change, it's a beautiful thing.
Thank God for change, I got a new name.

Thank God for change, it saved my life.
Thank God for change, Jesus paid the price.

Thank God for change, it is real.
Thank God for change, I know I'm healed.

Thank God for change, I'm not the same.
Thank God for change, it's not a game.

Thank God for change, I could have hurt somebody.
Thank God for change, when the days were cloudy.

Thank God for change, it's amazing to me.
Thank God for change, I've been set free.

Thank God for change, It's no longer hard.
Thank God for change, I could have had a charge.

Thank God for change, I see things different now.
Thank God for change, I can smile instead of frown.

Thank God for change, my future is bright.
Thank God for change, God showed me the light.

Thank God for change, I use to would get back.
Thank God for change, now I give it to God and relax.

Thank God for change, it doesn't matter if others can't see.
Thank God for change, just know it was done in thee.

Thank God for change, just repent if you slip.
Thank God for change, don't dwell on the guilt.

Carol Godfrey

Thank God for change, it's what grace and mercy is for.
Thank God for change, it waits for us at the door.

Thank God for change, one day it will all be over.
Thank God for change, when we leave here it will be all for His glory.

It's 5:25 a.m.

It's 5:25 a.m., and God has come on my side of the bed.
It's 5:25 a.m., and my flesh don't want to rise and be glad.

It's 5:25 a.m., just went to bed at 12:00 a.m.
It's 5:25 a.m., and He's messing with my head.

It's 5:25 a.m., He's singing, hands lifted, heart's open wide.
It's 5:25 a.m., and I'm trying to get some shut eye.

It's 5:25 a.m., I'm trying to roll out the bed.
It's 5:25 a.m., I'm coming, Lord, I said.

It's 5:25 a.m., time to hit the floor.
It's 5:25 a.m., don't want Him to knock anymore.

It's 5:25 a.m., He wants to get together.
It's 5:25 a.m., I can only imagine Him saying, "You know someone better?"

It's 5:25 a.m., it's been awhile since He called that early.
It's 5:25 a.m., the babies don't arrive until 7:30 a.m.

It's 5:25 a.m., Honey, "What's the urgency?"
It's 5:25 a.m., "Is this an emergency?"

It's 5:25 a.m., He wants to pray.
It's 5:25 a.m., okay God, you lead the way.

It's 5:25 a.m., as He started to lead.
It's 5:25 a.m., I started to receive.

It's 5:25 a.m., I'm ready now.
It's 5:25 a.m., so glad I didn't turn Him down.

It's 5:25 a.m., it's on now you'll.
It's 5:25 a.m., we having a ball.

Carol Godfrey

It's 5:25 a.m., we're on one accord.
It's 5:25 a.m., I know He's got more.

It's 5:25 a.m., praying for grace.
It's 5:25 a.m., to run the race.

It's 5:25 a.m., and He gives me the title to this book.
It's 5:25 a.m., I'm glad I got hooked.

It's 5:25 a.m., and I don't want to leave.
It's 5:25 a.m., Holy Spirit speak to me.

It's 5:25 a.m., and I need to catch Him while He's available.
It's 5:25 a.m., because before the day is over,
somebody needs to know He's able.

It's 5:25 a.m., it's a brand new day.
It's 5:25 a.m., and I really don't know what's coming my way.

It's 5:25 a.m., and I need Him to go before me.
It's 5:25 a.m., and I need to pray for my family.

It's 5:25 a.m., and He wants me to love on Him.
It's 5:25 a.m., and He wants me to hold Him.

It's 5:25 a.m., and He wants me to worship Him.
It's 5:25 a.m., and He wants me to praise Him.

It's 5:25 a.m., and He wants me to seek Him.
It's 5:25 a.m., and He wants me.

It's 5:25 a.m., and I want to enter into His glory.
It's 5:25 a.m., I wonder what it will be like in the morning.

It's 5:25 a.m., and I wonder will He let me rest a little longer.
It's 5:25 a.m., it doesn't matter because I'm growing.

It's 5:25 a.m., Thank You for choosing me.
It's 5:25 a.m., I made it all day because of Thee.

It's 5:25 a.m., my love, until we meet again.
It's 5:25 a.m., Thank You for grace and mercy, Your twins.

It's 5:25 a.m., Thanks for keeping me together.
It's 5:25 a.m., when the time comes, I'll see You in Heaven.

It's 5:25 a.m., until that day come.
It's 5:25 a.m., keep on coming in my room.

What Is A Friend?

(Dedicated to Sally Brooks)

I have a friend, who stuck with me 'til the end.
Check your circle; see if this is your friend.

I have a friend, when others thought I was crazy.
She never said, "Maybe!"

I have a friend, when they were laughing at my clothes.
She didn't stick up her nose.

I have a friend, when times got tight for me.
I know she went down on her knees.

I have a friend, when I need to move.
She got right in the groove.

I have a friend, when my daughter had to go to court.
She was there when others hoped the plan would abort.

I have a friend, when my air went out.
Her and her husband brought one to the house.

I have a friend, when the money got low.
She sowed a seed and told it to grow.

I have a friend, never expected anything in return.
She still hung out with me and we had fun.

I have a friend, she knew my struggle, which didn't matter to her.
She knew one day, Jesus would be my start.

I have a friend, she didn't tell my dirty business to others.
She knew some things I couldn't tell my brothers.

The Life of A Real Woman, Real But Healed

I have a friend, I'm not jealous of.
Because we serve the same God above.

I have a friend, when her truck broke down.
I took her my truck so she could still get around.

I have a friend, if I got it, she does too.
After all, that's what friends do.

I have a friend, who came to my rescue.
I want to know, do you too?

I have a friend, we go to the same church.
We used to go to one and got hurt.

I have a friend, who's sister passed away.
God gave her me; I think it's okay.

I have a friend, people didn't want her to hang around me.
Simply they knew I wasn't free.

I have a friend, I'm glad has a mind of her own.
She don't mind telling you, "I'm grown."

I have a friend, she's not wishy washy.
Will look at you and say, "Stop it!"

I have a friend, I described her well.
I know you're wondering if it's a male.

I have a friend, by the way she's a wife, a mother, and a sister.
I guess now you know, it's not a mister.

I have a friend, by the name of Sally.
A name sometimes used in pulpits,
but she's not the one your husband slept with.

I have a friend, she's family to me.

I have a friend, her realness comes from Thee.

Carol Godfrey

Check your friends, see if they are true.

Check your friends, see if they love you.

Check your friends, go through a test.

Check your friends, you figure out the rest.

Divorced Twice

Have you been divorced twice?
Wondering can you get it right?
Divorced twice, and it wasn't nice.

Divorced twice, and you want to belong.
Married people telling you to be strong.

Divorced twice, your bed lonely at night.
Trying to stay holy and it's a fight.

Divorced twice, it was supposed to be 'til death we part.
All you got was a broken heart.

Divorced twice, for better or for worse.
And all you got was hurt.

Divorced twice, you always the giver.
And all he knows is come hither.

Divorced twice, he was lazy on the couch.
And want you to be quiet as a mouse.

Divorced twice, he got another woman.
When he supposed to be your honey.

Divorced twice, you doing the best you can.
Only to find out you been had.

Divorced twice, you think something is wrong with you.
He just wasn't true.

Divorced twice, you just want to be loved.
He's in South Mills getting a hug.

Carol Godfrey

Divorced twice, didn't wait on the Lord.
All I heard was his noise.

Divorced twice, sent the papers in the mail.
Went to California and hauled tail.

Divorced twice, reversed the charges to me.
Because Cali set him free.

Divorced twice, after 3 months of marriage.
He was with Sister Mary.

Divorced twice, you feel like a failure.
They knew him but wouldn't tell you.

Divorced twice, everybody want to tell all now.
Why didn't you tell me when he was a clown?

Divorced twice, you can't buy love.
Real love comes from above.

Divorced twice, I learned to love me.
If we share love, we'll both be free.

Divorced twice, God had to work on me too.
If there's a next time, I'll know what to do.

Divorced twice, all three of us got it right.
Forgiveness for me was a fight.

Divorced twice, it wasn't all their fault.
My lust got caught.

Divorced twice, quick to get in bed.
Focused on the wrong head.

Divorced twice, you don't really know you.
How can you know the two?

The Life of A Real Woman, Real But Healed

Divorced twice, haven't had relations in years.
And God is keeping me still.

Divorced twice, God had to get all of them out of me.
So it could be just me and Thee.

Divorced twice, want to be loved right?
Seek the Light!

Love God with all your might.
Until then, stay in the fight.
And tell the pillow goodnight.

The Doors of Faith

(Dedicated to Apostle Moore and Elder Dot)

When I walked through the door,
Really, I had said, "Church no more."
Was looking for my place in God.
Didn't know it would be so hard.

All the other places I had been.
Didn't cultivate what God had within.
Wasn't trying to make friends.
Give me the Word and that's the end.

I thought Apostle Moore was like the others.
Found out he was a real brother.
Definitely didn't want to know his wife.
Had seen one, would cut you like a knife.

I was invited there by Prophet Perkins.
Found out it was a ministry for the hurting.
Began to hear the Word of God preached like I never heard.
My soul started soaring like a bird.

I kept going back, even when Satan wanted me to slack.
I found myself getting strong.
He was teaching how to lean on God's arm.

He never made it about himself;
Self was on the shelf.
God began to minister to me.
You're in the right door if you want to be free.

I was called to sing a song one day.
God was paving the way.
Saints, my heart was in a mess.
Went to The Doors of Faith and got blessed.

The Life of A Real Woman, Real But Healed

I had been messed over so much.
Had the mentality when ya'll gonna do such.

Apostle Moore didn't trust me and I didn't trust him.
Come to find out, we felt the same,
Because church people had been playing games.

My faith began to grow, after a few months in the door.
The Doors of Faith became a place like no other.
I had finally met some real sisters and brothers.

Found out Elder Dorothy was alright.
Her character proved to be tight.
I ended up on the praise team.
They found out God gave me the gift to sing.

I am so grateful and thankful for this man of God and woman of God.
My life is not as hard.
He prophesized I would write this book.
My God, my God. Look!

He helped push me to my destiny.
Cause all I wanted to do was sing.
Singing was all I thought there could be.
Until Apostle preached, *He's a God of Diversity.*

He's a God of so many gifts and talents.
I believe your name is on His ballot.
Find a man of God or woman of God who sees something in you.
And watch and see what God do.

God gets all the glory.
But thank you Apostle Moore and Elder Dot for letting me tell my story.
Couldn't tell the story without the two of you.
Thank you! Partners, I love you too.

Are You Pregnant Too?

There was a woman who found out she was going to have a baby.
It was Jesus' mother, Mary.

It was going to be a son, and He would be her special one.
So glad she agreed because her Son set me free.

Are you pregnant too?
And don't know what to do?
Found yourself in a mess, and don't feel blessed.

I've been there before.
I was supposed to have one more.
Scared, was supposed to be in school, instead skipped class, like a fool.

Started to get sick, and couldn't find Nick.
It was okay when I laid down, but now, here comes the clown.

When I told Nick, he said, "Oh, ****."
Told me we can't have this one. Oh, you know I was done.

I wasn't ready for a baby. Mama's baby, Daddy's maybe.
Couldn't tell Mom and Dad. They didn't like the man I had.

In fact, he had a girlfriend, a relationship he wasn't going to end.
After all, I fooled around with him, when my butt should have been in gym.

So now, I got to skip school again, because of what I'm carrying within.
He drove me to VA, I cried all the way.

He paid the price, even though it wasn't right.
I could have died on the table. I didn't know about God's favor.

Didn't know the identity. Often wonder if it looked like me.
That's something I'll never know, because I closed the door.
It's not a decision I'm proud of. Thank God for forgiveness from above.

The Life of A Real Woman, Real But Healed

I no longer carry the guilt or the shame,
For it's been covered under Jesus name.

He saw fit to make me a mother, so he gave me another.
She's my baby girl, so glad I brought her in the world.

Are you pregnant today?
And the father walked away?
Should I let the baby stay?
God will make a way.

Maybe you're feeling alone today. Look towards Heaven's way.
Bring that gift into the world. It just might be a baby girl.

Called Out

On September 11, 2015, God was up to something again.
Felt Him tugging on my heart. He was asking me to make a new start.

I was comfortable where I was. After all I was doing something I loved.
I had been doing it for 23 years.
What else could I do? Besides, I didn't have a lot of skills.

It was a rewarding job. Sometimes the clients could be hard.
I wanted to obey; yet, part of me wanted to stay.

Phyllis Creations was a nice atmosphere. It was just Phyllis and me.
We both got along well. We are both in Christ, I must tell.

Really didn't want to do hair all my life.
Didn't know it would be a pen and write.
God told me start paying off all your bills.
Take a sandwich to work and chill.

I told my clients this is it. They wanted to know who we going to get.
Some went to Phyllis and some went to others.
Maybe some went to Pastor Tyrone, my brother.

Regardless, I had to obey. Told my mother, she said okay.
Had a dinner for them all. I wanted to bless them for their loyalty,
great and small.

It wasn't an easy call. But had to trust God and stand tall.
There were days I wanted to go back. I sit still for 2 years,
wondering if I was on track.

I would pray, cry, and debate; and God would say, "Carol, just wait!"
Waiting on God isn't easy at all. People out there hoping you fall.

God would never tell her that. Even throw some Scriptures,
as a matter of fact.
Man don't work, man don't eat. I'm not Adam, I'm Eve.

You didn't ask them for nothing to eat. God said he would supply the needs.
If God called you out, step out. Forget the nay-sayers and the doubt.

Don't worry about what they say. Just let God have His way.

Don't you delete His call. God has something great, ya'll.
Trust His plan and His will. If you're not sure, be still.

Answer the call of God over everybody else. God will lead you to His best.
All God wants is a "Yes!"

H.S. (High School)

(Dedicated to Donna and Angel)

Classmates wasn't that great, a lot of girls were fake.
If you wasn't in their click, you were just another chick.

No nice shoes and clothes, they turned up their nose.
If you couldn't hang out all night, they laughed with all their might.

They had the good-looking boys, the other ones thought we were toys.
They had the good dates to the Prom. I was glad to have someone
on my arm.

Northeastern High School was great. My teachers, they were not fake.
My sport was basketball, as for cute girls, they walked the halls.

All they wanted to do was look, and see who they could hook.
I had to do my work, or Mom and Dad would be hurt.

I wasn't that smart, but always had a big heart.
Donna and Angel were my two girls. They were real, like pearls.

They treated me like I was somebody.
Made me laugh when days were cloudy.
We're still friends today. Graduation didn't cause us to go astray.

H.S. can be a joy or a low. Find friends who will help you grow.
Don't play around with your life, because your future is bright.

Learn all you can, because God has a plan.
Don't cheat your way through; do it God's way,
and you'll see graduation day.

Let's turn that tassel, and say, "Goodbye," to all the hassle.
And start your new chapter.

I did it, so can you too. Through Christ you can do it for sure.
All you need is a few, who believe in you.

Singing Comforts Me

Singing comforts me. It brings me to Thee.
It comforts me, when I can't seem to fall asleep.

Singing comforts me. God will give me a song.
It comforts me, when things seem to be going wrong.

Singing comforts me. When I feel alone.
It comforts me, when hope is gone.

Singing comforts me. When the bed is lonely.
It comforts me, you see I don't have a honey.

Singing comforts me. It's a gift He gave me.
It comforts me, that's how I get free.

Singing comforts me. It's my way of escape.
It comforts me, when I can't find my way.

Singing comforts me. When Satan gets on my nerves.
It comforts me, when life is throwing a curve.

Singing comforts me. When I'm in the shower.
It comforts me, every hour.

Singing comforts me. When I'm at an all-time low.
It comforts me, when I'm moving slow.

Singing comforts me. It calms my fears.
It comforts me, and dries my tears.

Singing comforts me. It touches my inner being.
It comforts me, it bring me healing.

Singing comforts me. When my heart about to faint.
It comforts me, and reminds my heart you can't.

The Life of A Real Woman, Real But Healed

Singing comforts me. When my body is going through.
It comforts me, and makes it new.

Singing comforts me. Because Jesus is mine.
It comforts me, it's my other lifeline.

Singing comforts me. Because He is my song.
It comforts me, all day long.

Singing comforts me. That's how He wakes me up.
It comforts me, that's His second touch.

Singing comforts me. When my grandchildren not around.
It comforts me, when I'm feeling down.

Singing comforts me. Cause I'm singing to Him.
It comforts me, because I know He's near.

Singing comforts me. It's second in my life.
It comforts me. Hallelujah, goodnight!

A Good Man

Sometimes, I ask myself, "Are there any good men left?"
A man, just for me.

A kind and gentle man. A man that will hold my hand.
A man who is faithful and true. Who doesn't want me and Sue, too.

A man dedicated to his family. Who prays until the Son sets us free.
A man who will tell the serpent to shut up.
Who will tell the devil or his Mom that's enough.

A man who will be on one accord, not one just keeping noise.
A man who has my back, when me, his wife, get a little slack.

A man who loves me for me, not looking for one trying to get me to sleep.
A man, not a boy, because I'm not a toy.

A man who will step up to the plate, when I'm short and the bills are late.
A man who will compliment me, on those days I don't feel like Thee.

A man who can keep his anger under control.
He'll say, "Baby, it's okay; let's roll."

A man who I can tell my secrets too, and won't judge me and say,
"I'm through with you."

A man who will love me 'til death, and love us, and not just self.
A man, we can pray together because I want to stay forever.

A man who God sends from above because I'm full of love.
A man that's been healed, that doesn't have a heart like steel.

Again, a man that's been healed, who Shelia tried to kill.
Finally, a man that's been healed, and I mean healed for real.

Love Me For Me

God had to teach me to love me.
I didn't know what love was supposed to be, until I found the love of Christ.
I thought the way I was doing it was right.

I thought love was, I do you, but not, you do me.
No wonder we couldn't agree.
As long as he's okay, this must be the way.

As long as you roll over at night, this is love and it's right.
As long as you can cook, then you think he's hooked.

As long as you are loving him, but he's giving his love to Kim.
As long as you're washing his clothes, but you're miserable, who knows?

As long as you're buying him things, but there's no commitment nor a ring.
So we settle for anybody, because at least I got somebody.

Because we don't think we're worth much, unless we're being touched.
And we won't walk away, because he knows just what to say.

But you don't really love me, it's what I do for thee.
I'm more than a bedroom and a couch.
When we learn what real love is, we'll open our mouth.

Love me, the good, the bad, and the ugly.
After that you'll find out I'm worth hugging.
Learn to love you before we say, I do,
Because after I do, you may find the real him and you too.

I Could Have

When I look back, God has been good to me.
I could have lost my mind, time after time.

When I look back, God has been good to me.
I could have been in jail, nobody able to post bail.

When I look back, God has been good to me.
I could have had AIDS, some things I've done, I can't tell.

When I look back, God has been good to me.
I could have died. I didn't know Jesus was on my side.

When I look back, God has been good to me.
I could have been killed, messing around because it was a thrill.

When I look back, God has been good to me.
Missed His call, because I wanted to have a ball.

When I look back, God has been good to me.
I could have cut some folks, just sick of their jokes.

When I look back, God has been good to me.
I could have cut somebody else life short.
His glory I would have aborted.

When I look back, God has been good to me.
I could have died on the abortion table.
I didn't know He was able.

When I look back, God has been good to me.
I could have missed out on my daughter,
She being raised by another mother.

The Life of A Real Woman, Real But Healed

When I look back, God has been good to me.
I could have missed out on my three grandkids,
Because of my life of sins.

When I look back, God has been good to me.
I could have lost my sight, because of not living right.

When I look back, God has been good to me.
I could have missed some birthdays, because I was living my way.

When I look back, God has been good to me.
I could have hurt my Mom and Dad, because I was acting bad.

When I look back, God has been good to me.
I could have lost my identity, because I just wanted to be me.

When I look back, God has been good to me.
I could have missed Jesus, the love of my life,
Because Satan knew my future was bright.

When I look back, God has been good to me.
I could have missed Heaven, because I thought the world was better.

When I look back, God has been good to me.
I could have missed joy, because I wanted to whore.

When I look back, God has been good to me.
I could have missed His mercy and grace.
And wouldn't have seen His face.

When I look back, God has been good to me.
I could have missed the streets paved with gold,
Because Satan and I had me on hold.

When I look back, God has been good to me.
I could have missed redemption, out here being simple.

When I look back, God has been good to me.
I could have lost my voice, living a crazy life by choice.

Carol Godfrey

When I look back, God has been good to me.
I could have lost my hands when God had this plan.

When I look back, God has been good to me.
I could have been in my grave, wouldn't be able to write and tell.

When I look back, God has been good to me.
I could have missed my destiny, because I wouldn't let Christ set me free.

When I look back, God has been good to me.
I could have looked back and went back.
But God, but God, kept me on track.

When I look back, God has been good to me.
I could have missed a good man in my life.
My Savior, my Friend, my Counselor, my Lord and Savior, Jesus Christ.

I looked back, it took me forward.
That's why you're reading my story.
And God gets all the glory.

My sisters and my brothers,
Look back to see how good God has been.
But don't' be like Lot's wife,
And want to stay within.

Go forward now, and leave all the clowns.
Reach for heaven, and get your crown.

Knock At The Door

There was a knock at the door.
Was already going through, what more?
Hadn't been home long, maybe it's Mom.
Whoever it was, please don't stay long.

I had just got home from work.
Been there half the night; my feet hurt.
I had been home about 30 minutes.
Saying to myself, don't people get it?

Was about to take a shower.
That day I had worked some long hours.
Heard Sierra call me. I said, "What do you want?"
Didn't know P.D. had a warrant.

She said, "Mom, it's the Po-Po."
I said, "I haven't done anything!" She opened the door.
The officer asked me, "Are you Carol G.?"
I said, "Yes Sir, that's me."

He says, "I have a warrant for your arrest."
Saying to myself, "This got to be a test."
I said "Sir, for what?"
He said, "Miss G., you missed court."

He asked, "Is this your child?"
He was very meek and mild.
I said, "Yes, Sir."
He said, "Step outside the door."

He didn't want to arrest me in front of CeCe.
Handcuffed me and downtown it was to be.
CeCe called Mom and Dad.
Dad came in looking mad.

Carol Godfrey

I was sitting in front of the magistrate.
Hands behind my back, singing, "I'm free."
I knew I had done nothing wrong.
That's why I could sing that song.

I had paid the parking ticket out of my pocket.
Come to find out they forgot to take my name off the docket.
So when they had roll call, I wasn't there and definitely wasn't in the hall.

I guess you know the rest.
The judge says, "Order for arrest."
It was an honest mistake. No reason to sue and take.
I was free and went on with my day.

Two Angels, One On The Way

I have two angels who are already free.
I have two angels who love me.
Two here God gave to me.
One in the womb I'm waiting to see.

Two here: 1 girl and 1 boy.
Yes, before you ask, they are grandma's joy.
Two here, one 12, one 8.
Sometimes they're not the best playmates.

Two here, who loves to play.
Don't matter, grandma seizes the day.
Two here, when they're not around it's lonely.
I pick up the phone and call my homies.

Two here, who are truly blessed.
Even they had some tests.
Two here, one was sick at birth.
Satan didn't want him on Earth.

Satan tried to take his breath.
If he took that, what was left?
He began to breathe on his own.
We were able to bring him home.

He's such a character when he imitates Barbara Jean.
He brings us laughter for real.
The other angel, she was my first.
Pleasant to the eyes at birth.
Had curly beautiful hair.
It didn't need a lot of care.

She is such a loving and caring child.
Praying God keep her meek and mild.

Carol Godfrey

Then there's the one in the womb.
Who will be here soon.
Can't wait for that first look.
Look at God, she made it in the book.

Not sure of her name yet.
Almost positive it's not Yvette.
The doctor said, it's a girl.
So that's what we're expecting. "Hello, world!"

Then it will be three.
The Father, the Son, the Holy Spirit, and me.
Hoping the womb will be free indeed,
Until a committed man get on his knee.

It's all good though.
Why, because my Jesus knows.
She has done no more than I did.
I just don't have the evidence of my sin.

Don't be hard on your son or daughter.
We are all counted as sheep for the slaughter.
Just encourage them to be all they can be.
Let go and let God set them free.

Love your grandkids as though you had them.
Because there's a foster child out there name Kim.

I Was Born Straight

I was born straight by the most powerful hand.
I did some things that brought guilt and shame.
And even though I've been delivered from the act,
Every now and then Satan tries to attack.

He tries to attack my mind.
So he can declare me guilty one more time.
Staying delivered is a fight,
Cause Satan don't want me to be right.

I put him in his place, Hell.
So God can give me a testimony to tell.
Let God deal with the spirit that's within you.
Homosexuality, lesbian, and gay are not our friend.

You are either male or female.
Adam or Eve.
There is no in between.

If you don't believe me and God in Heaven,
For the truth read Genesis Chapter 1 verse 27.

God created us in His own image.
Don't let Satan rob you of your privilege.
The truth of the matter is, maybe you tried something while in the world.
Whether with a boy like you, or a girl.

Maybe a brother, father, or uncle Sam touched you,
when no one was around.
It's not your fault, Satan wants to keep you bound.
Maybe you had a sexual fantasy, you and two more, or maybe three.
Let me tell you, God can make you free.

You don't have to struggle with your identity.
God made you the way He wanted you to be.

Carol Godfrey

Don't try to change what God made.
Ask God to put you together so you can worship and praise.

That's a part of life I'm not proud of.
But one thing I'm sure of, it's under the blood.
So when Satan try to remind me of my past,
I tell him I'm free and God has made me glad.

I struggled to write this part.
Because the world and Satan throw darts.
Especially when you speak from the heart.

You may not have tried some of the things I did.
But your lying, stealing, cheating, porn, and a variety of sexual
Acts, or even just thinking about it is sin.
If you don't believe me, read Proverbs Chapter 23 verse 7.
You'll find out none of us got it all together.

When you've been delivered and healed it doesn't matter anymore.
What matters to me is getting in Heaven's door.

So if this is you today,
Lift your heart and hands and say,
"Jesus, I'm ready for change; have Your way."

Take Time

Take time, and share your love.
Take time, it's a gift from above.
Take time, to hug your child.
Because they won't always be around.

Take time, to go out to school.
Take time, they are more than just rules.
Take time, to spend with your child.
Take time, everything doesn't require a dime.

Take time, they need our support.
Take time, or they will be in court.
Take time, teach them what's right.
Take time, teach them not to fight.

Take time, love them with all your might.
Take time, it's more than fighting.
Take time, stop yelling.
Take time, and tell them.

Take time, go on field trips.
Take time, or you will feel guilt.
Take time, eat lunch with them.
Take time, just you and Kim.

Take time, get off your phone.
Take time, as soon as they get home.
Take time, listen to them.
Take time, stop the deaf ear.

Take time, "How was your day?"
Take time, "Is everything okay?"
Take time, "What about school?"
Take time, check their mood.

Carol Godfrey

Take time, eat lunch at school.
Take time, even if you don't like the food.
Take time, go to events and games.
Take time, later there will be no shame.

Take time, take off work.
Take time, a few minutes won't hurt.
Take time, later may be too late.
Take time, ya'll bake a cake.

Take time, watch a movie together.
Take time, cherish the memory forever.
Take time, stop making excuses.
Take time, your excuses are useless.

Take time, don't miss the years.
Take time, later you'll be shedding tears.
Take time, when they get older.
Take time, they trying to hang with a brother.

Take time, it's not too late.
Take time, stop the wait.

Take time, so there will be no regret.
Take time, it's not over yet.
Take time, tomorrow may be too late.
Take time, seize the moment; it will be great.

I missed a lot with mine.
I didn't know the value of time.
Always had to work making a dime.
I should have took off and trusted Thine.

It doesn't take a lot.
Why don't you give it a shot?
Give them all the time you got.
Don't let Satan take your spot.

This is It

(Dedicated to Erthel & Edith Hines)

This is it, I told myself.
I was tired of life itself.
Daughter in school and,
Disobeying the rules.

Had to leave work,
Before somebody got hurt.
We found ourselves in a mess.
Didn't realize it was a test.

Wasn't rooted and grounded in the Word.
At this time, one foot in, the other in the world.
No wonder our life was upside down.
My faith wasn't on solid ground.

I was told I had crazy faith by Elder Darryl Banks.
As a matter of fact, my faith was losing rank.
Instead of my faith on promotion,
My faith status was demotion.

My faith was being kicked out.
So was my praise and shout.

I had taken enough.
Found out my faith wasn't so tough.
You think your faith is alright.
Then you find out it's not tight.

Called Mom on the phone.
Told her I need to get away from home.
"Carol, what's the matter?"
So much I couldn't gather.

Carol Godfrey

Got in my black Sebring one Thursday night.
Packed my bags and took flight.
Dropped my daughter off on Simpson Ditch Road.
Where I was going, they didn't know.

Headed to Greensboro, North Carolina.
I had arrived to the Hines' house, finally.

I was always welcome in their home.
A place of refuge when I needed to get gone.
I was depressed and oppressed.
Satan wouldn't let me rest.

I thought about staying there and changing my name.
He was really playing a mind game.
Then I heard the Lord speak to me saying,
"Get yourself together; get back to E.C."

I told the Hines it's time to go now.
I packed the black Sebring, headed to town.
I was glad to see my baby.
After all, it was just her and mommy.

Things began to turn around now.
God got my feet on solid ground. "Wow!"
Life was getting better for us.
I had to go through; guess it was a must.

Have you said, "This is it!"
And you're ready to quit.
So much going on in your midst.
Well get ready, life's about to shift.
And the glory of God is going to fit.

If this is you today.
Don't run away.
It's going to be okay.
Trust God for your day.
Be like Job, worship Him anyway.

Love You, My Brother

On March 23, 2019,
While I was out of town,
I was in Williamsburg,
A place you may never heard.

I was there with cousins, aunts, my sister, and Mom.
We had a family retreat.
Sharon, Phyllis, and Peaches decided we should meet.

It was nine of us.
Can you believe? Not even a fuss!
Didn't cost us a lot of dimes.
God is always on time.

God hadn't been long, got me up.
Time to worship and praise, the One above.
His Holy Spirit was high that morning.
All I had to do was step in His glory.

I had to step in while He as available.
I needed and wanted what was on the table.
I sat down at His feet.
That's the place He likes to meet.

That's okay with me.
After all, it's about Thee.
Got on the floor, I like that position.
It's a place of humility.

I didn't know a call was about to come through.
God had a plan, and only He knew.
My phone rung, who could this be?
With all these numbers calling me?

Carol Godfrey

I started to let it go to voicemail.
But I decided to answer instead.
It was my ex-husband number two.
Ya'll, my character has really grew.

He said, "You fell on my mind."
I guess he picked up the phone to see,
What he would find.
By the way, that was rather kind.

I asked about his wife.
After all, he has a new life.
The Spirit of God was upon me.
I was feeling really free.

The Lord said, "Tell him increase is on the way."
As a matter of fact, this was his day.
He said, "I receive it! I receive it!"
It wasn't coming from me, but from Thee.

I gave him what God gave me.
After all, it's God's will that we all be free.
I was in the closet, away from everybody.
Who I was talking to was for nobody.

Felt the Spirit leading me, end the call now.
So I began to come down.
Before I knew it, I said, "Love you my brother."
Remember, he's my brother-in-Christ; we're no longer the other.

When I would hear his name, it made me sick.
And I would make it known quick.
I couldn't let Satan have that hold on me.
For my heart needed to be free.

The call was ending.
But my lie was just beginning.
I'm a healed woman now.
Not one with a frown.

The Life of A Real Woman, Real But Healed

The next time your ex- call,
Or you see him in the mall,
Choose to be free that day.
Stop letting Satan have his way.

You are bound and so is he.
Let Christ in your heart and you both can be free.
Don't get to Heaven's door and He say,
"Depart from Me, you worker of iniquity."

I forgave him, and so can you.
My sister, my brother, it's the right thing to do.

"Are You Tired, Yet?"

"Are you tired yet?"
But you keep doing the same thing, I bet.
Moving in with men,
And saying, "He's my friend."

Friends don't sleep together.
Ask my friend, Jesus, in Heaven.
Don't ask Him for the truth.
Because He'll expect you to do.

First he leave boxers and shirts,
So he can come back and get under your skirt.
Don't give it up so quickly.
Get to know Mr. Mickey.

Stop settling for Mickey who don't have a job.
He's just a bed man with a hard.
After a while, you will get tired.
When your eyes come open, my child.

Don't he have a place of his own?
Tell him you don't mind being alone.
When you feel it's going too far,
Kindly escort him to his car.

It's time my sisters stop living below who we are.
That life won't take you far.
It's time sisters to take our time.
Let's get ourselves together; stop looking at his dimes.

Stop looking at the car.
Can you see his scar?
Let's stop looking at his body.
Find out if there's a Holly.

The Life of A Real Woman, Real But Healed

"Aren't you tired of his cheating and lying?"
Tell Satan you're not buying it.
Aren't you tired of him shoving you around?
Sound like to me he's a clown.

Come on sisters and brothers, let's wait.
Let's take our time and date.
Take me out, bring me back home.
It's okay for us to go in the house alone.

If he don't call you on the phone,
Just because you sent him home,
That lets you know he's a boy,
And haven't grown.

He'll lay there as long as he can.
Satan knows you won't take a stand.
Don't you want Dad or brother to give him your right hand?
Well, come to Jesus because only He can.

Don't be a live-in-friend.
You're worth commitment and a ring.
You're worth a diamond and so much more.
Sisters and brothers let's get ready for the sanctuary door.

"Are you tired, yet?"
Rise to God's standard and be blessed.
Don't put your life on hold.
Come on out as pure gold.

A Book in Her

I saw a book in Shakia G.
I couldn't see a book in me.
Apostle Moore spoke it so many times.
I just couldn't grasp it in my mind.

Then one Thursday night Prophet George was speaking.
The Word that night started leaping.
I felt like Mary, Jesus' mother.
God said, "Here comes another."

I said, "Here comes another; another what?"
He said, "Another book to be read."
I said, "Lord, Is it really me?" He said,
"Yes! Carol, write! Set my people free."

I talked to God all the way home.
I was like, "God, I've done so much wrong."
He said, "You have to be strong."
He said, "Just lean on my arm."

I thought about Matthew, the tax collector,
Who got up from his booth.
Took a ink pen, some paper,
And wrote a book.

He left everything behind to follow Jesus.
God was saying, "What's your reason?"
"God, I really don't have one."
He said, "Trust Me and My Son."

God has no respect of person, this I know.
Here's the book to prove it so.
Shakia G. is my sister, this is true.
We had to do what God call us to.

The Life of A Real Woman, Real But Healed

Often times we see things in others.
Like our sisters and brothers.
Only to overlook what God has within.
Because we're so busy looking at next of kin and sin.

If you can always see, it may not be God.
Most things He ask, I find it hard.
If He told you too, it won't come back void.
We got to just trust God.

Whatever He called you to,
He'll pave the way; you just move.
He's got great things for you.
Get under a shepherd who will help push you through.

There's something great in all of us.
Ask God to pull it out, it's a must.
He wants to birth Him out of you.
Cause when He birth, it's all good.

He can take the bad and the ugly,
And turn it into great mercy.
We haven't done anything so bad,
That our God would turn His head.

Ask God to look way down today.
And if you're ready,
Ask Him to have His way.
God wants to make your day.

Don't let what you been through define what He made.
Because what He made was great.
He knew you before the womb.
Fulfill His purpose, don't take it to the tomb.

Don't die outside your dreams.
Because God wants to fulfill,
Just seek His will.
It may require being still.

Carol Godfrey

There's something in you.
Maybe a book, CD, or a theatre play.
All I know is it's something great.
In due season, it will come your way.

Move forward like I did.
There's a lot of dreams within.
Look to Christ our friend.
Every beginning has an end.

The End

There's an end to everything.
Whether sun or rain, hurt or pain.
There's an end to everything.
Arrival date and departure date.
Every life, God's going to rate.

Don't know where mine is on His scales.
All I know is He told me to tell.
I want His glory to outweigh my story.
Without Him, life is boring.

I hope my life will balance out before the end.
And He'll say, "Well done, my friend."
I will fall short from time to time.
I will repent and God will get me back in line.

See what's unbalanced in your life.
Maybe an attitude or a lie.
Get on God's scales, He'll make it right.

Maybe you hurt somebody today.
Get on the scales and lose the weight.

See what's unbalanced in your life.
Ask God to help you make it right.
He wants to give you an expected end.
Like a mother waiting for child within.

Life can be like a car out of line.
When we're out of line, our God don't shine.
The car begins to go all over the place.
Come on, take your rightful place, grace.

Where you've been is not the end.
Where you going is great, my friend.

Carol Godfrey

Be like an eagle, soar high.
Tell your defeats and failures, bye, bye.

Your end is your beginning.
When you get to the end,
That's when Jesus steps in,
And gives you a new start, my friend.

See yourself as a success.
Let God uncover the rest.
God wants to give us His best.

See after we get sick and tired as we say,
That's when God says, "Now do it My way."
You see, He's the beginning and the end.
So let it go and new life will begin.

He gave David and Bathsheba a new start,
Because David was after God's heart.
They ended up with another child.
Remember, their other child died?

You see, it wasn't the end for them.
And you are no different than him.
If He did it for them, watch Elohim.
Rise up and touch the hem.

The woman with the issues of blood at her end.
Her new life was getting ready to begin.
Her 12 years was about to be over.
Come on my sister, she was about to see His glory.

Just when I thought it was the end,
As you read, my life was full of sin.
Committing the same sin over, and over again.
Would Christ give me a new beginning.

I started seeing the end.
And found out Satan was not my friend.
That's when life started again.
Get ready, it's not the end.

Don't let Satan tell you it's the end.
Get in His presence, you will win.
There's a conqueror inside of you.
Stir him up, what I just said is true.

God's not through, you have more to do.
You know it's true.
That's why you're still here.
You know what I just said is real.

I Didn't Want To Know

I didn't want to know Him.
I didn't want to be free.
My life of sin felt great to me.

I didn't want to know,
The man on Calvary.
Just let me do me.

Let me go to church, sing in the choir.
Only stay there for about an hour.
I didn't want to know His power.

My baby brother tried to talk Christ to me.
Leave me alone, I didn't want to know Thee.
As a matter of fact, he would call home.
On the table I would lay the phone.

When I thought he was finished.
I would say, "Okay bro, I got to go."
He would say, "Okay, I know."

He told me, "I'm going to send you a tape."
Oh no, just let me hang out late.
In church, but I was a fake.
Trying to fake until I make.

I didn't want God to clean me up yet.
Had a few more males to get.
I didn't realize my reputation was at stake.
I didn't care; I thought the world was great.

I didn't want to know Him, just my friends.
After all, they hung with me 'til the end.
I didn't know the place called Hell, but it was real.
I thought the preacher was cussing still.

The Life of A Real Woman, Real But Healed

I thought to myself, He's no better than me.
Why I need to know Thee?
I didn't' know I was a sinner in need of mercy.

I know a lot of people, after all, from Elizabeth City.
Most people knew the Baileys and Godfreys.
Some people thought we were perfect kids.
Some did in the open, some of us hid.

I didn't want to know Him; too complicated.
Just let my life be X-rated.
He was too perfect for me.
Why would He want thee?

I didn't want to know Him; He requires too much.
And I wasn't ready to give Him such.
He was too righteous for sister girl.
I didn't want Him in my world.

I didn't want to know Him, too much work.
After all, I thought salvation was going to church.
Let me do my thang, and Jesus you do your thang.
But we're not going to hang.

I didn't want to know the cross,
Because I couldn't be the boss.
Just let me run the streets.
And maybe someday we'll meet.

I didn't want to know Him; too holy for me.
I wasn't ready to climb to reach Thee.
Let me stay on my ground.
Maybe I want to be found.

I didn't want to know Him, leave me alone.
After all I am grown.
I didn't know I was a fool.
A fool who needed to be schooled.

Carol Godfrey

I didn't want to know Him, He was special.
What He want with me, I'm hateful.
I didn't realize I was missing the greatest man.
And all I had to do was take His hand.

I didn't want to know Him, stop chasing me.
I thought I was free and He couldn't see.
I didn't' realize this man loved me.
And all He wanted was to set me free.

Do you know Him today?
Don't be like me and run away.
Come on home,
Because you're not grown.

Do you know Him today?
He's really special in all His ways.
Why don't you choose Him today?

You'll be glad you did.
He just wants to be your friend.
Don't be like me.
The man just wants to set you free.

Freedom is a good thang,
Because my God reigns.
He reigns over everything.
This is true. Let Him reign over you.

Holiday Inn

Went to the Holiday Inn, me and my boyfriend.
You know what I went to do. It wasn't to tie his shoe.

Hadn't been long got saved.
As you know my fornication wasn't in the grave.
My flesh said feed me, and of course, I agreed.

Stopped by J.C. Penny to see Elder T.J. that night.
He said, "Sis, you alright?"
I said, "Why you ask?"
He said, "What you up to tonight?"

I said, "Going to get my groove on."
I knew by his eyes it was wrong.
He said, "Carol, you're a mess."
I said, "Say what you may, my flesh getting blessed."

Told him I'm not there yet. Pray for me.
I went out the door, being Satan's whore.

I wasn't a whore that walked the street.
But a whore under the sheets.
Reminds me of Gomer, Hosea's wife.
Fornication was her fight.

God told him buy her back.
By this time she wasn't worth much, right?
But God can change anybody, and make them somebody.

We got to the Holiday Inn, planned to stay all weekend.
Until Sunday morning, that was not morning glory.

Pulled the sheet back, found something in the bed; it wasn't crack.
I said, so and so, is that a bug?
God had left a sign: the bug, not a hug.

Carol Godfrey

I didn't understand the signs and the wonders. I was trying to get under.
God was telling me go home, but this flesh was strong.

Called the clerk at the desk.
Come check the room so I can rest.
Didn't realize it was a test.
Giving that up was for everybody else, not myself.

Now the bug has gone away, and I'm still trying to stay.
My flesh was going to find a way.
God trying to tell me, not today.

Getting ready to do my thing, now my man acts like a clown.
Do C.C. know I'm in town.
Man, I'm trying to get busy; who in the world is she?

My flesh is mad now, my hind pots cold.
I'm packing, heading for the door.
I told him can't believe you asked me that, right in the middle of the act.

I got up and went home, and left him there alone.
Got in my Camry and I was gone.
Guess God was happy I didn't get none.

He told me he was sorry. And I said see you tomorrow.
Went on home, he did too.
Didn't get to do; wasn't supposed to.

I didn't know about deliverance yet. Something I needed to get.
It was definitely a struggle. Satan wanted to keep me in his huddle.

They said, "He was a keeper."
Okay, let me try and see.
It's been 15 years now, no man can say He had me.
Don't think Satan doesn't desire me.
Because he doesn't want me free.

God has kept me strong.
I have to pull on His arm, or I may commit wrong.
I know I have to stay in His palms.

The Life of A Real Woman, Real But Healed

Yes, my flesh rises sometimes. And I have to tell it, "No!"
And tell Satan where to go.
Because who God made me has to show.

When you are sold out to God,
Don't let nobody tell you it's not hard.
You have to ask God to guard you.
Or you'll find yourself where you started.

Remember, we reap what we sow.
If I was you, I'd close that door.
Ask God to kill your flesh, so God can give us His best.

You're more than a bed and sheets,
And Satan's piece of meat.
You're more than a hotel. Let God clean you so you can tell.

You're more than cheese and wine.
You're more than bed time.
Don't fall for the trap. Don't be like Eve and get got.

We can't be wise in our own eyes.
Jesus is all wise, my child.
Satan knows how to smooth talk. Put your heels on and walk.

If you're not married, stay out that hotel and motel.
God wants to give you a testimony to tell.

If the man thinks you're all that, then he won't run around like a rat.
He'll know you're a good catch.
You'll be at the altar and that's the end of that.

55, It's Time

55, It's time, it's time to release the book He had in me.
It was time to tell all, from the greatest to the small.

55, It's time, to release somebody free; somebody who struggled like me.
Someone who was afraid to open up, so you kept it shut up.

55, It's time, to release the hurt and pain, also the guilt and the shame.
It's time to release the captive free, so you can have God's great mercy.

55, It's time, to release all the weight, and the things God hate.
It was time for me to tell the world regardless of race,
every boy and girl.

It was time for me to release single Moms.
All those the devil had harmed.

It was time for me to release single Dads,
Who got involved with needy women and got had.

It was time for me to release those dead things in my life,
So Jesus can make it right.

It was time for me to release that husband,
So get healed before another.

55, It's time, to release that child, give them to God and smile.
It's time to release that bad relationship, take God's hand and get a grip.

55, It's time, to release that spirit of molestation.
People just taking and taking.
It's time to release that porn, or God's going to sound the horn.

55, It's time, to release that lying and stealing, stop hurting and killing.
It's time to release that fantasy; it's time to be free.

The Life of A Real Woman, Real But Healed

55, It's time, to release that lust. It's not an option, it's a must.
It's time to release that rage. We're too old for that at our age.

55, It's time, to release that scheming. It's time to touch His hem.
Your scheming will find you out. Your shout is not what it's about.

55, It's time, to release those drugs. Let God, He wants to give
you a big hug.
Let go of that needle. Go home to your family and mingle.

55, It's time, to release that adultery, leave that man alone
and his family.
Don't be the reason he left home, because one day,
you look, and he's gone.

55, It's time, to release that achy heart. Let God heal every part.
So we won't hurt others who had nothing to do with it, my brother.

55, It's time, to release that song, take your place, it's where you belong.
Don't worry about the money; God's source is never funny.

55, It's time, to release your Mom and Dad, stop walking around mad.
Satan wants you to be sad, but God wants you to be glad.

55, It's time, to release that ex-wife, make amends, and stop the fighting.
Let's tear the devil's kingdom down. Who wants him around?

55, it's time, to get ready to go home. Jesus is waiting on the throne.
Is your name on the roll for our Heavenly home?

55, it's time, to get ready to know where you're headed.
Your life is not over; God still wants to get His glory.

Don't waste another minute, second, or hour.
Be overtaken with His power,
He has much in store for you this very hour.

55, It's time, it's time to get this in the heart.
It's time, it's time, get on your mark.

Carol Godfrey

55, It's time, it's time, get ready, set, go.
It's time, it's time, run to the door.

Don't miss God's timing for your dreams and visions.
Be quick on the mission.

I'm Free Now

Some will criticize my life and my book.
See, you don't know what it took.
The purpose was to catch a fish on a hook.
Reel them in and let Christ cook.

It took a yes from my heart.
In order for me to start.
And it's God I came to please.
It's not for people who don't see a need.

So when you get on the phone and laugh,
All I care is I made Him glad.
I'm free now, so I can't worry about the clowns.
I'm glad to be the talk of the town.

This was God's mandate on my life.
What's in your life? Have you got it right?
There's some things in us that needs to come out.
So, really, you need to shut your mouth.

I'm not afraid anymore.
It's about one or two coming in God's door.
You didn't choose me.
Christ died so I could be free.

Satan nor you can't hold my past anymore.
I know that for sure.
See, repentance from the heart.
Gave me a new start.

Everybody wants to stay in the closet.
Because the world and saints are heartless.
What happened to building people up?
If that's not you, then shut up.

Carol Godfrey

How do you think artist got where they are?
Even some of them came out the bar.
Listen to the words of their songs.
You'll find out they also did wrong.

Just because they got a mic now,
Some of them used to be clowns.
Some even messed around,
While they were out of town.

You know the song, He Thought I was Worth Saving?
The key word is "He" is the one who gives grace.
What have you buried lately? So don't start digging.
At least mine isn't hidden.

He set me free so I could help somebody else.
Don't want nobody to go to Hell; because you see, I care.
Some people when you open up, were looked at differently.
Get to the point, you don't care about either.

They said all manner of things against Jesus.
Mighty funny, you need Him to be free?
He's the one who paid the bond,
For all of our wrongs.

If it wasn't for Him, we all would be bound.
Like a dog tied to a tree, looking around.
Waiting on his master to come home.
Loose him so he can roam.

All the things I revealed had me bound.
I'm free now, right here, in my hometown.
God looking for real saints. Rise, shut the devil down.
So if you hear my name, say, "Stop it now!"

I'm free now, don't do me no harm nor danger.
Christ died for me and laid in a manger.
There was no room in the Inn.
Don't even curse my next of kin.

The Life of A Real Woman, Real But Healed

I'm free now, be happy for me.
Don't let nobody tear my testimony.
Tell somebody this girl passed the test.
Put their down-talking to rest.

Have you been made free like me,
But can't tell and be free indeed?
Stand up to Satan, tell him to leave.
Send him to Hades and be free.

Praying for you, my sister, my brother.
I don't need to know your name.
I pray for deliverance, every day,
In Jesus name.

I pray for the things he brought me through.
I know there's a you, and you out there, too.
Be free now! Who knows, one day I may be in your town.
And we can talk about how God carried our sins in a hearse,
And put them in the ground.

"He's My Everything Now"

"He's my everything now," my best friend.
He stuck with me until the end.
When in His arms, I'm safe from harm.
Can't let go, want to hold Him long.

"He's my everything, now."
It's a song I sing.
I'm His wife, with a covenant ring.
I sleep with Him every night.
Without Him, loneliness is a fight.

"He's my everything, now."
I can't get enough of Him.
With my nasty self, He let me touch the hem.
God made me whole.
He brought me out as pure gold.

Like a criminal in jail,
Hoping somebody make bail.
So see, they're not really free.
Until they're declared not guilty.
So glad He paid the ransom for me.
"He's my everything, now."

"He's my judge."
When my life was full of sin,
He threw out everything.
He wiped my slate clean.
Like Ruth, now I can gleam.

"He's my source."
When I couldn't find no help.
I wanted to depend on someone else.
I found out He was great.
My God, is not a fake.

The Life of A Real Woman, Real But Healed

"He's my healer."
When I was sick.
He was my doctor like no other.
He stuck closer than a brother.
Healed all my wounds, and did it real soon.

"He's my protector."
When I was out there doing my thang.
He watched over me while I wanted to hang.
He kept me from disease ya'll.
AIDS, gonorrhea, syphilis, He kept me from all.

"He's my keeper."
When I desire to hold a man's hand.
Or sleep with one because I can.
But, because I'm committed to Him,
The sheets not worth the guilt.

"He's my bridge over troubled waters."
When there was so much trouble in my life,
Some my fault, some not.
Jesus, now I got.
Found out who my friends were not.

"He's my bread."
When guilt and shame tried to starve me.
Hoping I wouldn't survive.
God sent a word, His bread kept me alive.
It's he that's causing me to thrive.
He's my everything, now.

"He's my water."
When sin was trying to drain me.
Satan was hoping, God, don't reign.
Went to the well to see the man.
He gave me water, I'll never thirst again.
He's my everything, now.

"He's my Lord and Savior."
When I didn't want His ownership,

Because I had so much lip.
Didn't' want to give in.
Now, He's my Lord, Savior, and friend.

"He's my Father."
When I thought Albert was enough.
Until Satan started throwing his stuff.
Didn't think I needed another father.
Until God took Albert a little further.
I found out He'll never leave me.
He's a real father indeed.

"He's my joy."
When I thought I couldn't take no more.
My joy was out the door.
I found the man who gives joy forever more.
He's my joy in sorrow.
And always my hope for tomorrow.

"He's my peace."
When Fathers, ex-husbands, friends left me,
Couldn't find no peace within.
All I had was stress.
When would peace be on this test?

I knew He was the answer.
Stress was trying to kill me like cancer.
I found the peace-maker.
The One sitting in Heaven.

"He's my strength."
When life was sucking everything out.
Even praise, worship, and shout.
And you're wondering all about.
Just breathing but not alive.
No strength, and you want to hide.
Then you find out His strength is like no other.
And that He wants to be your covering.

"He's my morning glory."
When I lay down at night.

The Life of A Real Woman, Real But Healed

Tired of the daily fight.
When will the story end?
Because I know Satan not my friend.
Then I realized tomorrow will be a different story.
Because He's my morning glory.

"My King of kings."
I found out He's better than anything.
He's the voice I sing.
He's better than a Rolls Royce.
He's my choice.
I tried a lot of things.
But now, He's the King of kings.

"He's mine now."
So glad I let Him in.
I claim Him as my King.
He's my everything.
I can tell Him anything.

Can tell Him my secrets.
Because really, nothing is hidden.
"He's mine now."
He has the right to mess around.
It's my soul He found.

He can be at my house and yours too.
Don't have a problem with that, He's Lord.
There's enough of Him to go around.
So, stop acting like a clown.

"He's mine now."
But we can share.
We don't have to be jealous.
He's an awesome fellow.
He wants to be your everything.
Whether it's sunny or rain.
Whether hurt or pain.
Down or low, don't you know.

Carol Godfrey

He wants to be your everything.
He don't want you to lack anything.
Because He can do all things.
If you let Him be your everything.

Crazy Faith

(Dedicated to Elder Darryl Banks)

Elder Banks told me about crazy faith.
Faith that makes sense to nobody else.
Faith that's always put you to the test.
It's a faith that never seems to rest.

A faith Satan can't shake.
Crazy faith is what it takes.
This book is the evidence of that faith.
It molds and then it makes.

Elder Banks said, "Put it on your car."
Crazy faith took me this far.
This is not the kind you put in a jar.
This is the kind of faith you keep in your heart.

Crazy faith makes you look stupid.
It's like an arrow in cupid.
It's the faith you step out and do.
Don't matter who's not with you.

Crazy faith makes people talk.
It will make your friends walk.
This faith will make Satan stalk.
He will watch you like a hawk.

Crazy faith I know sounds ridiculous.
Get some crazy faith, it's a must.
It makes the devil hush.
Drive it like you in a rush.

Crazy faith makes you reach.
It will take you to your highest peak.

Carol Godfrey

With this faith all you need is Thee,
Because God holds the master key.

Get some crazy faith like I did.
This kind of faith can't be hid.
It's faith like when you were a kid.
It's the kind we all need.

Faith you thought you could do anything.
Like jumping off a moving swing.
This kind of faith you need wings.
Soar you like an eagle, the sky is the end.

Crazy faith takes you to the top.
A devil in hell can't make you stop.
This kind of faith leaves a mark.
Are you ready to start?

Get ready, get set, go!
Why you moving so slow?
Crazy faith moves you to the door.
It tells you God got more.

Don't be afraid of the heights.
Just know crazy faith is right.
That's right, God is the light.
Pursue your dreams with all your might.
Tell little faith, goodnight.

Elder Banks, "Thank you for the prophecy."
Here's the fruit off that tree.
I praise God for thee.
For God using you to speak to me.

Holler or Yell

Communication is not a holler.
It's a place I choose not to follow.
It was done to me.
I turned around and did it to C.C.

There wasn't a quiet voice.
Just a lot of screaming and noise.
That could be heard all out doors.

It was shut up and sit down.
Or you got from Dad a bad frown.
And you knew he wasn't fooling around.
Like Barney, the clown.

It left a bad taste in my mouth.
Because all I knew was a shout.
They wanted me to be quiet like a mouse.
After all, it was their house.

It wasn't called child abuse.
It came from their generational roots.
And they needed to be loosed.
So did my sister and brothers too.

Every now and then it rise up in Mom.
And I know she doesn't mean no harm.
But regardless, I know it's wrong.
So, through Christ, Satan I have to disarm.

Jesus didn't holler or scream.
He speaks the Word and that's what He means.

Nothing gets accomplished this way.
Really didn't hear a word you said.

Carol Godfrey

Because you were so mad.
And all you did was made me afraid.

Why didn't you just sit me down.
And say, "Let me talk to you, my child!
Baby, what you just did was wrong.
Why couldn't you be calm?"

I guess you didn't know how,
Because you weren't taught yourself. "Wow!"
I'm just grateful I know better now.
So, I can teach Ayden and Miyah how.

I know it's a process.
And sometimes it's going to be a test.
Help us, Lord, to put it to rest.
I believe in the end they tried their best.

Parents stop yelling at them all the time.
That's why some kids commit crimes.
Open up the communication lines.
Be a psychiatrist sometimes; won't cost you a dime.

That's why our children talk to others.
Because they can't relate to their father or mother.
You're so busy hollering and yelling.
Sit down and listen, carefully.

Stop making them afraid of you.
Learn to love them through.
If you don't know how, ask God to show you.
That's how Jesus grew.
His Father didn't yell or holler.
He taught Him what He knew.

So, lower your voice.
You'll be glad you made the choice.
Your child is a gift from above.
Not a sound proof board.

The Life of A Real Woman, Real But Healed

Holler back at me if this is you.
Shout glory, Hallelujah! It's true.
Yell it out of your mouth.
Cause you know, I'm right.

The Thief

I used to be a thief.
Until I met the Chief.
I would go in the store.
It's not in E.C. anymore.
Take clothes and so much more.
And push the cart right out the door.

I gave away most of the things.
Wasn't saved then, so I felt no shame.
Me and my friends saw it as a game.
God won't let me reveal their names.

We would get a storage tub.
Fill it with baby clothes, even rugs.
Not realizing we were acting like thugs.
People who rob and mug.

We could have went to jail.
Stealing, my parents not going to do bail.
They told us, "Go there, you're on your own."
No need of asking to use the phone.

A security guard saw me one day.
He told me, "I saw you, gonna give you a break."
"Don't come in here no more and take."
"Going to take you down to the place."

I knew he meant business.
Don't be dumb, Carol, and don't listen.
You going to be in handcuffs.
Keep thinking you tough.

You better quit while you're ahead.
Going to find yourself in the slammer instead.

The Life of A Real Woman, Real But Healed

Want to be resting in your own bed.
Maybe sleeping on the floor instead.

I could have had a record.
To get one, only takes seconds.
That follows you around for life.
Unless you got a lawyer that's tight.

What I was doing wasn't right.
I was in the hair business, money wasn't tight.
Had money in my purse.
Wrong, thinking nobody getting hurt.

It's just stuff, so I thought.
Who cares about the law.
I'll never get caught.
I'm glad the security guard saw.

He saved me from jail,
And putting my family through hell.
That's why now I can tell.
All my dark secrets, God paid the bail.

Don't judge the inmate behind bars.
Maybe you didn't steal, but left someone scared.
In God's eyes, that's a crime.
Don't have to be in prison to do time.

True repentance can erase the charge.
God is a good lawyer, He'll never be barred.
Why not hire Him today.
Only He can wipe the charge away.

Don't carry the guilt and shame around.
Let them talk in your town.
Tell them I was lost but now I'm found.
And what I did, I'm no longer bound.

Carol Godfrey

You may not have stolen out of a store,
But stole your friend's husband and more.
Stealing is stealing in God's eyes.
See, I'm willing to tell you mine.

Realness is on my life.
So I can help somebody in the fight.
Because none of us got it all right.
Or we wouldn't need Jesus, the light.

The truth exposes darkness.
Truth is a matter of the heart.
It's truth that gives a new start.
All you got to do is your part.

So, whatever you stole,
Admit it, you'll come out whole.
I choose to be bold.
To Christ, not you, I'm sold.

All Messed Up

You probably say she was all messed up.
Probably sounded like I was no hope.
How in the world did this woman cope?
I found Jesus and that's no joke.

Messed up was the truth.
Staying messed up wasn't going to be my roots.
It was time for me to choose.
Or I was going to lose.

You see, God specializes in mess.
It's people who don't want you blessed.
They want you to flunk the test.
So you can't receive God's best.

God wanted somebody like me.
I had to choose to be free.
Because my life was on Messed Up Street.
It was Christ I needed to meet.

I was headed down the wrong road.
Going where I don't know.
It sure wasn't Heaven.
You see, my mess, was that little leaven.

It was that lump of dough.
You put it in your mouth and say, "Oh, No!"
I don't want no more of this.
Like tasting lumps in your grits.

Most people don't know all my mess.
So I know this book will tell the rest.
But make sure to tell God has blessed.
It's for His glory, nothing less.

Carol Godfrey

My mess is out the closet.
God wanted it for a deposit.
So just take it all in.
Like the song, you will win.

Don't try to hide your mess.
Confess and get blessed.
That's what I've done.
I'm no longer on the run.

Bring your mess to the table.
The God I serve is able.
He can turn around your mess.
Let Him show the world you're blessed.

It will catch up to you after a while.
You will cry instead of smile.
God wants to use you for His glory.
Give Him your messed-up story.

Mess means all over the place.
You can't successfully run the race.
Too many obstacles in the way.
Give God your mess and have a blessed day.

Word of Life

(Dedicated to Beryl Combs)

Word of Life, a church in Chapanoke,
Where I found Jesus, the man I know.
Was invited there by Beryl Combs.
This is the place I got reborn.

I was sitting in the back one night.
The Spirit of God was really high.
Elder Banks started to prophecy.
I was scared, I closed my eyes.

I was a babe in Christ.
Thought those tongue talking people weren't right.
I wanted to get out of sight.
You see, I knew my life was tight.

I thought it was a cult.
This church I was ready to abort.
If I get out of here tonight.
I know I'll be alright.

Beryl didn't tell me what to expect.
I felt like an ant, the insect.
Let me get out of here.
My heart was full of fear.

I came out of a Baptist church.
None of that was happening.
This was all new to me.
I thought Beryl set me up for real.

Carol Godfrey

She invited me to Delaware one weekend.
Beryl said, come on, go my friend.
Told her I'll think about it.
It was E.C.S.U. day in the city.

I decided, well, I guess I'll go.
She probably thought I'd be a no show.
I surprised her that night,
And showed up at the site.

I got on the bus.
The bus driver act like he was in a rush.
"What's the hurry?" I said to myself.
God had something for me on His shelf.

The anointing was there.
I was a babe, what did I care.
I didn't' know what it was.
So, why all this noise.

I had on a pretty red dress.
But inside I was a mess.
Jesus was about to be my guest.
Let me tell you what happened next.

Something hit me in my soul.
And it really took hold.
I started shouting all over the place.
Was I inside Heaven's gate?

I remember hitting the wall.
But yet, I didn't fall.
I went shouting some more.
They had to walk me out the door.

Got on the bus, "Drunk," as they say.
And been running for Jesus since that day.
I found the Man that's so great.
All my sins, He washed away.

The Life of A Real Woman, Real But Healed

Asked Pastor Whidbee to baptize me.
He said, "Okay, Sis. Godfrey."
He asked when I wanted to go down.
I said, "Can I go now?"

Pastor Whidbee didn't care about time.
He was concerned about souls, not dimes.
He would get right out his bed.
"It was all about Jesus." He said.

He and Elder Ferebee got the water ready.
My heart filled; feet seemed unsteady.
Mama Mute singing and praying.
Time to go down in Jesus name.
With her, this was no game.

Came up giving God the praise.
That's the day my name changed,
From sinner to saint.
The devil, I ain't.

So glad Beryl invited me.
I was a woman in need.
A woman needing to be free.
From Satan who had me bound to him.

"Thank you! Word of Life."
It was there I found the light.
My life has not been the same.
Through the ministry, I found Jesus name.

"Thank you! Word of Life."
I now have my sight.
As Mama Mute say, "It's tight, but it's right!"

There's a word for your life.
If you're not saved, get it right.
Jesus may come for you tonight.
He's coming like a thief in the night.

Baby Jordan

(Dedicated to Azayiah Jordan)

Baby Jordan made it here.
Now I'm the grandmother of three.
One boy and two girls,
Who God allowed in this world.

I was hoping she'll be here before the book.
It was a C-section, it took.
My daughter couldn't have it on her own.
She needed a push from the throne.

It doesn't matter how she arrived.
As long as Jesus, the Surgeon, was the guide.
Yes, praise God, Dad was by her side.
Smiling like he was the child.

Praying he'll be a good Father.
And don't see her as a bother.
I believe he will do the right thing.
Because this grandma will take him to Jesus name.

Welcome, Baby Jordan.
I will treat you just like the others.
Samiyah and Ayden Godfrey,
Your sister and brother.

I guess you're the last one.
Sierra told me she's done.
She had her tubes tied.
No more replenishing for her on this side.

Three different nations now.
On my knees I must bow.

The Life of A Real Woman, Real But Healed

All kinds of personalities.
God, pray for me.

Grandma got your back baby-girl.
Just embrace my love and my hug.
They will come from God above.
Pure and clean, agape love.

I welcome you here.
You are someone dear to me.
Just like Ayden, Samiyah, and Mommy.
You're all a gift from Thee.

You're a branch added to the tree.
Jesus, the Vine, connected us three.
Welcome to the families.
The Jordan's and the Godfrey's.

"Thank you, God, for a safe delivery."
"Thank you, God, for grace and mercy."
"Thank you, God, for your forgiveness."
"Thank you for doing it for me!"

I give you all the glory.
Even Baby Jordan will have a story.
I will tell her, it's all for your glory.

Singleness

A life that don't shine that bright.
A life that's lonely at night.
A life that can be sad.
A life wondering, where's the man?

Everybody telling you hold on.
Married women saying, stay strong.
You look, there's a man on their arm.
I know they mean no harm.

A life, in every season, can be cold.
Wishing you had someone to hold.
But you still in the Potter's mold.
When it's finished, only He knows.

Wanting to go to the park.
Hoping things don't go too far.
Hoping he'll respect your walk.
Don't need the smooth talk.

Wanting to be kept by God.
Let's be real, singleness is hard.
You see married couples holding hands.
And you hear God sayings, "Stand!"

I look at Raymound and Neicy,
And know what marriage should be.
Speaking kind to one another.
Hey God, "Do you have another of them brothers?"

Watching them laugh and play.
And all you want is a date.
And someday, a wedding cake.
But first, I need a soul mate.

The Life of A Real Woman, Real But Healed

Watching him look in her eyes.
And she gives him this big smile.
And your mind wondering what's tonight.
Smile ladies, you know I'm right.

Watching him open the door.
Your heart saying, "I can't take no more."
All you desire is a walk on the shores.
God, "do you have anymore?"

Neicy and I were on the back porch.
Talking about the Lord and more.
Raymound comes out the door,
Looking for the one he adores.

His heart wondering where she was.
Found her outside with cuz.
Cuz has to look at all of this.
Devil tell you, look what you miss.

Yes, I am saved.
But my flesh try me some days.
Then Jesus say, it's going to be okay.
Just let me have my way.

Singleness is a fight.
But holiness is right.
Trying to hold on with all your might.
It's just you and Jesus again tonight.

Can I get a witness out there?
Singleness makes you feel bare.
Make you feel like Eve.
Stripped of you leaves.

God is telling you cleave, cleave, cleave.
And flesh saying, I got needs.
Can I get a witness out there?
Like Delilah in Sampson hair.

Carol Godfrey

God, don't you care.
He says hold on anyway.

Can I get a witness out there?
You see other singles doing their thang.
Because of the call, you can't hang.
On your flesh, He reigns.

The devil telling you, one time won't hurt.
Then the Prophet spot you in church.
Because you laid down with Curt.
Now your flesh want to curse.

Can I get a witness out there?
I told you I would be real.
Because I know how you feel.
But thank God I'm healed.
Until marriage, my body, is sealed.

Only He can enter in.
Because He's my beginning and my end.
And because I am His,
Me and the sheets can't be friends.

The oil on our life cost too much.
For us to do such.
So, Satan, Lucifer, hush.
Singleness, for now, is a must.

The Baby of Five

I'm the youngest one.
After me, guess Mom said I'm done.
Was ordained to be a girl, not a son.
Just grateful God let me come.

Mom had a hard time with me.
That's what Aunt Lois and Mom told thee.
Guess she paid the price for it to be.
Satan didn't want me free.

They said I was a big baby.
Causing a lot of pain in her labor.
I wasn't born on the operating table.
Found out, they weren't able.

I was born in the house.
Doctor didn't get to hear me shout.
Mom had a mid-wife.
Because times were tight.

They weren't making a lot of money.
But she had Albert, her honey.
Didn't matter to her.
She just needed to give birth.

The cost was very low.
So Mom said so.
Maybe 40 or 50 dollars.
Not today, somebody holler.

Aunt Lois said Mom didn't even cry.
Didn't make not even a sigh.
Told me, Mom was a tough woman.
She just wanted me to come.

Carol Godfrey

Five is the number for grace.
And grace is what it takes.
Having a baby is not a piece of cake.
So, Father's step to the plate.

You don't have to stay with your girl.
But stay in your baby's world.
Whether it's a boy or a girl.
Remember, you laid down with Cheryl.

Labor is not a joke.
It's not like a coke.
Take a swallow and burp.
Labor really hurts.

It's really a matter of life or death.
Fathers, Moms need your help.
The baby can't help itself.
I know this for myself.

Labor is more than just a push.
If ya'll had one you'll know what it took.
Ask Mary, Jesus' mother.
The Holy Ghost was with her like no other.

Joseph was a good Step-Dad.
He helped take care of the baby Mary had.
He didn't leave her alone.
While she laid and groaned.

Jesus knew ya'll couldn't bear the pain.
So He made woman, that's how He came.
Respect the Mother of your child.
God loaned them for a little while.

Mothers, let Fathers see their child.
And watch your child smile.
Let Jesus be your guide.
Stop being on Satan's side.

The Life of A Real Woman, Real But Healed

Put "you" to the side,
It's about your child.
Stop telling lies.
They will find you out after a while.

They will come to know the truth.
Then what you gonna do,
When they turn on you?
Now you're left with a boo, hoo.

Too late to cry,
When they start asking why?
Why you keep him from me?
After all, he loved thee.

Oh, that day will come.
They won't always be in your home.
That's why there's the telephone.
Hi Dad, it's Tyrone.

Why you leave me?
Mom wouldn't let me see thee.
Had no money for a lawyer.
I'm sorry my daughter.

My Dad was there for me.
Until God set him free.
He took care of all five of us.
On him, my Mom could trust.

Your child is a gift from above.
All they want is kisses and hugs.
Throw that division under the blood,
Because Jesus is love.

Love conquerors all things.
Come on Moms and Dads, let Jesus reign.
Stop doing your own thang.
It's about L.J., Shawn, and Kane.
So, stop causing the child pain.

Anxiety

It's a spirit of fear, and it tries to stay near.
What's not supposed to be, so we can't be free.

It's facing the unknown. Anxiety, be gone!
Leave us alone. God we need the throne.

It will make you cry. Feel like you about to die.
God don't feel nigh, cause fear standing by.

You can't sleep, and sometimes, can't eat.
It consumes your life, both day and night.

Anxiety is a fight. A silent killer out of sight.
I know this to be right. Somebody say, "But Christ."

I walked this fleshly thang. It robs you of so many things.
Things that are dear to you. And people have no clue.

Doctors want to dope you up, just so you can cope.
Anxiety leaves you no hope. It causes you to just mope.

You feel like a zombie, don't feel like thee.
Want to stay under sheets. Nobody you want to greet.

I need to tell the story about God's giving glory.
Lori had long beautiful hair, every strand seemed to be there.

She was diagnosed with cancer, and her hair had to answer.

Was supposed to do it the next day. My mind said, "No way."
Fear came over me, as the day came near.

It wasn't a day of being glad because my heart was very sad.
She told me what the doctor said, with the devil I was mad.

The Life of A Real Woman, Real But Healed

Her hair would come out, wanted to scream and shout.
It would fall down the drain. Anxiety makes you feel insane.

I couldn't imagine that day. My heart fainted away.
Anxiety met me the day before. Found myself in Alvin's door.

I set in his barber chair. Anxiety was having its way.
But he and Rob took care. Anxiety isn't fair.

I passed right out. Nothing coming out my mouth.
Rob picked me up, and put me in his truck.

Took me to the hospital. Anxiety had me.
So it wanted to be. Medicine don't make you free.

It only calms you down, but inside there's still a frown.
Even when someone's around, you're off the Babe Ruth mound.

When you feel it coming on, know that you're not alone.
Tell anxiety to be gone. Give it to Jesus on the throne.

Now take a deep breath. Ask God for help.
You are not alone. Let prayer be your phone.

Get Jesus on the line. He'll come through every time.
Won't have to spend a dime. Tell anxiety, peace is mine.

Put anxiety in park, not in your heart.
Put peace in drive. Come on Sis, Bro, let's ride.

Gout, But Got To Go

Woke up this morning, toes feeling funny.
But got to make that money, because bills still running.

What could this be, my foot is not free.
Can't even touch the sheet, they feel like heat.

Went to work anyway. Can you imagine my day?
But it was about hair, my feet didn't care.

I had to go to work, even though my feet hurt.
Clients depending on me, and the Benjamins I need to see.

I had a child to feed, plus we had other needs.
It was just her and me, so feet, you have to carry thee.

So, I walked on the side. The pain I couldn't hide.
It was painful for sure. No insurance! "What can I do?"

I finished the day out, really don't know how.
You know the clients were proud, and my feet speaking, sit me down.

Went to "Walk-in" doctor, couldn't wait until tomorrow.
Hurt so bad, wanted to holler. I was calling on the Father.

Walked in the place, looking for relief today.
In those places you have to wait.
Don't know how long it's going to take.

Took one look at my foot. His head he shook.
He already knew. I was one of the few.

He said, "Miss G., you have rich man's disease."
I thought it was just a tease. Had never heard that before.
And wanted it no more.

The Life of A Real Woman, Real But Healed

Gout, too much acid in the blood stream.
Eating food I thought I needed.
Like shell fish and caffeine. Gout is not my thing.

Needed to change my diet. Gout felt like fire.
Feet swollen and red. Hurt to even touch the bed.

Put me on one crutch, I didn't get around much.
Hurt even to touch, but still went to church.

Propped it on a chair. Knew Christ would be there.
He died for my foot. Faith is what it took.

I no longer eat red meats, can't stand the heat.
I rather have free feet. I got a shout to keep.

I could praise with one. Satan didn't have my tongue.
Jesus just that kind of Son. But gout, it's no fun.

Are you in pain today?
Jesus can wash it away.
All you need is faith, and His amazing grace.

Stay away from those foods. You know you should.
Do you want the meat or some shouting feet?

Tell gout, get out! Not welcome in my house.
You're trespassing on God's property.
Now lift those hands and praise Thee.

The Closet

In the closet at home, praying to my Father on the throne.
That was our place to be alone, away from child and phone.

It was a walk-in-closet; I needed to talk to God, the Father.
Just like Mary and Martha, crying out for their brother.

While in prayer and praise I heard the voice say,
"Preach my Word!" Was that what I really heard?

I cried even louder trying to drown out His power.
He spoke it again. I wasn't ready to give in.

I kept on praying. He kept on saying,
"Preach my Word!" He knew I heard.

I wasn't deaf or dumb, just didn't want to come.
I just did understand the Bible. Preach your Word? How?

I said, "I don't know enough about You."
Most of all, I wanted to be true.
Didn't want to be a fake. Real, just like my Mom's pound cake.

If I wasn't going to give my all. I didn't want to accept the call.
Call somebody else. But not me, myself.

He said it one more time. "Preach my Word!"
Now, I can't ignore what I heard.
He said, "You hear Me, baby girl."

Why you select me? After all I've done to Thee.
Who could I set free? Then He said, "Carol, let me use you."

I finally said, "Okay, Lord!" But giving in was hard.
I finally broke down, and was ready to be crowned.

The Life of A Real Woman, Real But Healed

I felt a peace come over me. The answer, "Yes," set me free.
All was for Thee, and not for me.

Under Bishop Gregory leadership, I knew we needed to meet.
The Spirit said, "Call on the phone."
Part of me, hoping he's not home.

He answered the phone. He didn't ask what's wrong.
He said, "I already know." I need not say no more.

I'll never forget that day; Jesus was going to have His way.
Regardless of what I said. He said, "Hey Carol, I'm the head."

Then He said, "You can't out talk me. I'm the Shepherd;
you're the sheep. You will be mine.
Through you, my glory will shine."

As He continued to speak, He said, "All you've done against me,
was just a closet ministry.
I hung on the Cross. All your sins, I brought."

Finally, He said, "The reason I brought you out, so others
will know what I'm about.
Closet ministry, you can't hide, it will find you after a while."

We are given a choice. Listen to the voice.
Will it be Christ today or will you walk away?

Put on your best, don't dress like the rest.
Let him dress you from the throne.
Put your spiritual clothes on.

You may not be a preacher.
You may not be a teacher.
You may be a gate-keeper.
But all got a closet ministry.

God brought you out of something, now you get to running.
Pull somebody else out; after all, that's what the gospel is about.

Carol Godfrey

It's not about fortune or fame.
It's about spreading His name.
It's not the Wheel of Fortune game.
It's about from whence you came.

Satan hope you bankrupt.
Closet ministry shuts him up.
When you come out the closet,
Satan's no longer your father.

Time to land on victory.
So start your closet ministry.
The Son wants to set you free.
So tell defeat, not me.

Start your closet ministry today.
Give all your sins away.
All it takes is faith.
And the rest is history. Okay!

The Power of Forgiveness

There's power in forgiveness, it's the only way to be healed.
Without it the soul dies. You need to get it right.

I know you're innocent, and saying, "Why me?"
He/she did it to me. It don't matter, just get free.

You going to need it later. Ask Bathsheba and David.
Who committed adultery, but through forgiveness is free.

Even though, there was a penalty.
But forgiveness also brings mercy.
Ask Adam and Eve, who ate off the wrong tree.

They tried to cover themselves.
They should have looked for God's help.
It takes denying yourself, that's the first step.

Yes, he did it to you. The facts are true.
And everybody else knew, and bitterness, it grew.

You can't stand her guts, but you're the one in a rut.
She's gone on with your man. They're walking, holding hands.

You lapping your eyes, while they laugh and smile.
Don't go to Hell behind them. Forgive that man and Kim.

So you can get on with life, that's what it's all about.
There's some women in prison, for this exact reason.

Killed a woman behind a man. She locked up and he got Cam.
Don't have to be you, because the Word is true.

"Don't forgive others," Jesus said.
It's in the Bible, in red.

Carol Godfrey

Read Matthew Chapter 6 verse 15.
Is that what you see?

I know what I'm talking about. You can't shout it out.
It has to come out of mouth. I'm trying to tell you how.

I saw my first husband at the park, sitting in his Honda car.
I had just come from church. Yeah, my heart, he did hurt.

He paid the price too. That I made for sure.
I tried to rip his head off for breaking my heart.

Jesus said, "Today Carol, it's time to jump this barrel."
This was a big barrel for me. Help, I needed help from Thee.

I asked him to forgive me, and he accepted my plea.
He said, "You alright!"
I said, "No, got to get it right."

We started laughing about the past. You know Satan got mad.
He might as well be glad, because I did what God said.

Un-forgiveness has power over you. In your spirit it takes root.
Then other things attach to it, like envy and hatred.

Don't let Satan do this to you. Release yourself and him too.
It's time to grow up in Christ. Come on sisters, make it right.

We wrestle not against flesh and blood.
Un-forgiveness is a spirit, have you heard.
Let's tear Satan's kingdom down. Who wants him around?

He doesn't play fair. In fact, he doesn't care.
He wants you on his side. Let Jesus be your guide.
Drop your pride on today. Tomorrow may be too late.
Put un-forgiveness in the grave. Bury it for your sake in Jesus name.

Put un-forgiveness to rest. Go ahead girl, pass the test.
God wants to give you His best. Put un-forgiveness to death.

Revenge

Revenge is his name. Get back is his game.
You want to play, that's fine. Revenge is mine!

Before I got saved, my boyfriend, you don't lay.
Hide and seek was a game, but not with my name.

He was supposed to be playing ball. Other girl had made a call.
I was home in the bed. My flesh not dead.

Heard he was messing around. I live in a small town.
A lot of people knew me. It was going to be me or she.

I had heard where she lived. My flesh couldn't be still.
Got out of my bed. Got in my Honda, it was red.

Called a buddy on the phone. He knew something was wrong.
I said let's ride Clyde. I didn't waste no time.

I went up the lane; going to win this game.
I had no shame. Revenge was my name.

You playing around on me. You got the wrong she.
I didn't roll like that. Tonight, you're going to get it, Jack.

He was standing under the garage. My heart he tore apart.
She's leaning on him. They didn't know I was near.

He said, "It's not what you think."
I said, "Well what I see stinks."
You're supposed to be with me. Who is she?

I was through talking now. You silly clown.
You will ride back cold. Revenge had me sold.

I busted his windows out. Miss prissy running her mouth.
I told her, "You better go in the house, and be quiet as a mouse."

Carol Godfrey

This is between me and him. In revenge, you don't see so clear.
You did it to me. You're not going free.

Free was too easy, and you cheated on me.
"Oh no, brother! You'll think before you get another."

He had me arrested that night. What I did wasn't right.
I should have kept my cool. Revenge said, "Get that dude."

He knew what he had done. To the police station he comes.
Came to bail me out. They took word of mouth.

Promise to come to court, or my freedom they would abort.
Now, I'm playing the game, talking sweet to the man.

Hoping he'll drop the charge, for damage to his car.
Had to sweeten him up, trying to save my butt.

It worked ya'll. Now, I got the ball.
I scored on this one. I must say, "It was fun!"

Revenge is a terrible thing. It's not worth your name.
As a matter of fact, a deadly game. That only brings along shame.

Don't try to get back. Let God take up the slack.
"Revenge is mine." Said the Lord.
Tell revenge get out the door.

Get yourself together.
Get your eyes on Heaven.
Ask Jesus to help you.
He's faithful and true.

Let God deal with enemies.
You just watch and see.
Don't rejoice over their defeat.
You just pray for thee.
God bless you, be free.

Surprise

(Dedicated to Phyllis Brooks)

On May fourth, twenty-nineteen, God had a surprise for me.
Something I never had before, on the other side of Apex door.

I absolutely had no clue, so surprised, didn't know what to do.
Seems like my feet were glued. My mouth, wide open too.

Nothing ever of this magnitude. God so faithful and true.
Through Phyllis, He came through. I'm 55, this was new.

Talk is a cheap thing. Walking it is the real thing.
Phyllis, to God, I bless Your name. It wasn't for fortune or fame.

God has an appointed time, for His glory to shine.
Just be faithful and kind. You may be next in line.

Never had "surprise" anything, just a cake and ice cream.
Thank God for that too. But show me something new.

When I walked in, I saw family and friends.
Where do I begin? I didn't want it to end.

All walks of life, black and white.
Such a beautiful sight. What Heaven will be like.

Trina, Karen, and Paige. It didn't matter the age.
It was for V.I.P. (Very Important People). People close to me!

Thought it was for my daughter; not for the Mother.
That's what I was told. I was totally sold.

It was a setup from above. The real gift, the gift of love.
Love from my sister, Phyllis. No details did she miss.

Carol Godfrey

Everything was just beautiful. Red, white, and purple.
The food looked good. Potatoes, chicken, string beans too.

I cried the whole time. I couldn't wrap it in my mind.
The season was Thine, and God was shining.

They prayed over me. My soul was already free.
Felt running in my feet, but weak in my knee.

The feeling I couldn't explain. My God chose me to reign.
He thought that much of me. Really, He's the V.I.P. to thee.

Everything in me shut down. All I felt was the glory cloud.
If He doesn't do anything else. He surprised me before I left.

I didn't have to wait to see it in Heaven's gate.
Got a glimpse what it will look like, when God crack the sky.

He's coming like a thief at night, wrong or right.
That's not a might. Oh, what a sight!

It won't be a "surprise." Your soul will rise.
In Heaven or Hell. Your life will tell.

But until that day comes, enjoy the "surprise" and have fun.
It will happen for you. No respect of persons, it's true.

You're on God's mind. It's a matter of time.
The Son will shine, and you'll hear. "Surprise!"

A day you won't forget. It will be the best.
God hears your cry. He's on your side.

Enjoy the moment of the day. A surprise is coming your way.
God has a plan, because He's the man.

Just keep being you. God is not through.
He won't miss a thing. After all, He knows your name.

About the Author

Prophetess Carol Godfrey was born and raised in Elizabeth City, NC to the late Albert Godfrey and Mother Edna B. Godfrey. She has one daughter, Sierra, and is a grandmother of three, Samiyah, Ayden, and Baby Jordan. She is a called out 23 year cosmetologist, single mom, divorced twice, sister to a sister, two living brothers, and one deceased. Prophetess Godfrey is a praise and worship leader, intercessor, and minister of the Gospel. This is the life of a real woman, real but healed. Woman of God! To God be the glory.

www.ingramcontent.com/pod-product-compliance
Lightning Source LLC
Chambersburg PA
CBHW081746100526
44592CB00015B/2312